BIRD WOMAN
SACAGAWEA'S OWN STORY

as recorded by
James Willard Schultz

Mountain Meadow Press

BIRD WOMAN: SACAGAWEA'S OWN STORY
as recorded by James Willard Schultz

Based on the Houghton Mifflin Company 1918 edition of
Bird Woman (Sacajawea) The Guide of Lewis and Clark.

Cover photography by Lynne Marie Whisner, Moscow, Idaho.
Cover art by Edgar S. Paxson, from the 1912-1919 series.

Schultz, James Willard, 1815-1947.
    Bird woman: Sacagawea's own story / James Willard
Schultz.
    p. cm.
    Previously published by Houghton Mifflin, Boston, under
the title Bird woman (Sacajawea): the guide of Lewis and
Clark. 1918.
    Includes index.
    Preassigned LCCN: 98-67701
    ISBN: 0-945519-23-0

    1. Sacagawea, 1786-1884. 2. Lewis and Clark Expedition
--(1804-1806) 3. Shoshoni women--Biography. 4. Shoshoni
Indians--Biography. I. Title.

F592.7.S12 1998   978'.004974'0092 [B]
                                   QB198-1279

TABLE OF CONTENTS

NOTE

For many years following the Lewis and Clark expedition, Sacagawea was duly thought of as a heroine and even, by many, as the true guide of the Corps of Discovery. Much art and literature was composed to laud her spirit of adventure, her courage and her leadership role in the expedition. Familiar nineteenth century statues, for example, show her with right arm held up, finger pointed, guiding the explorers westward. Historical research has since demonstrated that, indeed, she did not lead the Corps or serve as key guide, but rather played a vital role in its survival and, in one instance, in the survival of its records. The following poem, which hails the heroine in a fashion typical of the day, appeared as a preface to Schultz' original 1918 book.

SA-CA'-GA-WE-A
by Edna Dean Proctor

Sho-sho'-ne Sa-ca'-ga-we-a — captive and wife was she
On the grassy plains of Dakota in the land of the Minnetaree;
But she heard the west wind calling, and longed to follow the sun
Back to the shining mountains and the glens where her life had begun.
So, when the valiant Captains, fain for the Asian sea,
Stayed their marvellous journey in the land of the Minnetaree
(The Red Men wondering, wary — Omaha, Mandan, Sioux —
Friendly now, now hostile, as they toiled in the wilderness through),
Glad she turned from the grassy plains and led their way to the West
Her course as true as the swan's that flew north to its reed nest;
Her eye as keen as the eagle's when the young lambs feed below;
Her ear alert as the stag's at morn guarding the fawn and doe.
Straight was she as a hillside fir, lithe as the willow-tree,
And her foot as fleet as the antelope's when the hunter rides the lea;
In broidered tunic and moccasins, with braided raven hair,
And closely belted buffalo robe with her baby nestling there —
Girl of but sixteen summers, the homing bird of the quest,
Free of the tongues of the mountains, deep on her heart imprest,
Sho-sho'-ne Sa-ca'-ga-we-a led the way to the West! —
To Missouri's broad savannas dark with bison and deer,
While the grizzly roamed the savage shore and cougar and
       wolf prowled near;
To the cataract's leap, and the meadows with lily and rose abloom;
The sunless trails of the forest, and the canyon's hush and gloom;
By the veins of gold and silver, and the mountains vast and grim —
Their snowy summits lost in clouds on the wide horizon's rim;
Through sombre pass, by soaring peak, till the Asian wind blew free,
And lo! the roar of the Oregon and the splendor of the Sea!

Some day, in the lordly upland where the snow-fed streams divide —
Afoam for the far Atlantic, afoam for Pacific's tide —
There, by the valiant Captains whose glory will never dim
While the sun goes down to the Asian sea and the stars in ether swim,
She will stand in bronze as richly brown as the hue of her girlish cheek,
With broidered robe and braided hair and lips just curved to speak;
And the mountain winds will murmur as they linger along the crest,
"Sho-sho'-ne Sa-ca'-ga-we-a, who led the way to the West!"

THE NAMES

The following table of names is provided as a reference. Several persons in BIRD WOMAN are known by more than one name. In the top list, the names after each colon are aliases.

Names With Aliases

Sacagawea:
>   Tsaka'-kawia or Bird Woman
>   Bo-i'-naiv or Grass Woman,
>   Bah-rai'-bo or Water-White-Men Woman,
>   Wad-zi-wip' or Lost Woman
>   The Gentle Woman
>   Led-the-First-Big-Knives Woman

Mrs. James Kipp: Sak'-wi-ah-ki or Earth Woman
Hugh Monroe: Mah-kwi'-i-pwo-ahts or Rising Wolf
Lewis and Clark (or white people): Long Knives
Meriwether Lewis: Long Knife
William Clark: Red Hair
Four Bears: Ma-to-to'-pa
Crow Woman: Is-sap-ah'-ki
Hardesty: Terrible Tongue
Heavy Robe: Never Talks
Black Bow: Cameahwait

Names Without Aliases

Lone Otter	Red Eagle	Rock
Lone Walker	Red Shield	Black Cougar
Black Horn	Toissaint Charbonneau	Drouillard
Rattle Woman	Big Man	Red Eagle
Mink Woman	Elk Horn	Black Bow
Black Lance	Otter Woman	Big Man
Red Crow	Leaping Fish Woman	Diving Eagle
Red Arrow	Baptiste Charbonneau	Middle Sun
White Grass	Little Otter	Big Cottonwood
Deer Robe	Heavy Robe	Little Mountain
Black Horn	Red Willow Woman	James W. Schultz

INTRODUCTION

It is night. Light from a small campfire flickers against the elkhide walls of a tipi in which you sit. Ready for an evening filled with tales of bygone days, you nestle into the warmth of a buffalo robe. Quiet chatter ripples through the circle of friends with whom you sit, glowing coals casting rosy light on your faces. Then he begins, one of the West's greatest storytellers, James Willard Schultz, speaking fluently in the tongue of the Blackfeet Indians.

His tale will transfer you in place and time to a Mandan village along the Missouri River sometime during the first quarter of the nineteenth century. There his almost-mother Earth Woman and friend Rising Wolf, a trader, listen intently to an earlier storyteller, a Shoshone Snake woman living with the Hidatsas, or Minnetarees, who had captured her following an attack on her own people. The Shoshone woman tells of her experiences traveling from Mandan country to the Pacific Ocean and back with the Lewis and Clark expedition in 1804-1806.

To the Minnetarees this storyteller is known as *Tsaka'-kawia*, Bird Woman. To her people, the Shoshone Snakes, she is *Bo-i'-naiv*, Grass Woman. After her capture by the Minnetarees, the Snakes also referred to her as *Wad-zi-wip*,' Lost Woman; and still later, following her adventure with Lewis and Clark, they called her *Bah-rai'-bo*, Water-White-Men Woman. Yet history will record her name as Sacagawea, and her journey with Lewis and Clark as the expedition of the Corps of Discovery.

Thus this book relates Sacagawea's own account of her capture by the Minnatarees and of the Lewis and Clark expedition. First, however, it explains how her story came to be told to Earth Woman and Rising Wolf in the lodges of the Hidatsas and later, in the 1880s, retold to young James Willard Schultz by those who had heard Bird Woman, Sacagawea, speak. Thus, what follows includes the retelling of Sacagawea's account of the greatest expedition in the history of the United States.

PART I

HOW BIRD WOMAN'S STORY
CAME TO BE TOLD

Chapter I

Earth Woman and Hugh Monroe

Away back in the 1870s, fired with boyish zeal for great adventure, I, James Willard Schultz, went from New York to Fort Benton, Montana, to see something of life on the buffalo plains. It was my good fortune to fall in at once with the late Joseph Kipp, the most noted Indian trader of the Northwest. His mother was a full-blood Mandan and widow of Captain James Kipp, American Fur Company doctor in the Mandan village in 1821. I later lived with my new-found friends for many years, and a nomadic life it was. Wherever buffalo were most plentiful, there we were; some winters living and trading in the lodges of the Blackfeet and other winters in hastily built but comfortable log trading posts which we put up here and there.

In my way of thinking, it was an ideal life that we led. Wherever we roamed, from Canada south to the Yellowstone and from the Rockies far eastward upon the plains, we felt that, in common with the Blackfeet people, the country was ours, all ours! No part of it had as yet been ploughed or fenced, and Fort Benton, at the head of navigation on the Missouri, was the only settlement upon it. During the busy season from October until spring, I helped in our trade with the Blackfeet tribe for their buffalo robes and furs. At other times, I hunted with my Indian friends, and even, on several occasions, went to war with them against other tribes. It was all great — life on the buffalo plains!

The evenings were as full of quiet enjoyment as the days were of exciting adventure. With each setting of the sun came storytelling time, and around the lodge fires or before the mud-daubed fireplaces in our rude posts, the people gathered to smoke and eat broiled buffalo tongues and in turn relate weird tales of the gods, tales of war and hunting, and of far trails, all the various happenings which

3

made up the history of the past. Were the narrator Mandan or Arickaree, Blackfeet or white man, the conversation was always in the Blackfeet tongue. I soon mastered it and was always called upon to contribute my share to the evening entertainments. And thus it was that I got from my almost-mother, Mrs. Kipp, and her equally aged companion, Crow Woman, and Hugh Monroe [*aka* Rising Wolf], and Black Horn, an old Gros Ventre warrior, some interesting tales about Sacagawea, heroine — yes, savior — of the Lewis and Clark Expedition, and other tales about the two great leaders and some of their men. But before relating them, I must say a few words about the narrators themselves.

Mrs. James Kipp, Sak'-wi-ah-ki, Earth Woman, had been born in 1803, a daughter of Ma-to-to'-pa, Four Bears, one of the Mandan chiefs who welcomed Lewis and Clark to the Mandan villages in 1804. Before and after her marriage to Captain Kipp in 1821, Mrs. Kipp often heard Sacagawea relate tales of her adventure on the trail to the Western sea and back. And from her father and mother and others, Mrs. Kipp got the story of the coming of the first Long Knives, Lewis and Clark and their men, to the Mandan country and of their experiences there.

Is-sap-ah'-ki, Crow Woman, was an Arickaree, and was born in the village of that tribe located on the Missouri some distance below the Mandan villages. The two tribes were at times united in defense against their enemies, the Sioux, Assiniboines, Crows and others, and so, from earliest childhood, Is-sap-ah'-ki and Sak'-wi-ah-ki were playmates and firm friends.

Soon after she was married, Crow Woman went out on the plains with her man and a small party on a buffalo hunt. They were attacked by a war party of Crows and all killed except Crow Woman, who was captured by the leader of the Crows and became one of his wives — his slave wife. The Crow never treated her unkindly, but in the many years that followed, her one desire was to return to her own people. When at last the opportunity came, she escaped from the Crow camp only to fall into the hands of a war party of the Kai'-na, a tribe of the Blackfeet, and its leader, Lone Otter, made her his third wife. More years passed and then one spring when the Kai'-na came to Fort Benton to trade, Crow Woman heard Mrs. Kipp speak to her son in the Mandan language and ran to her, stared at her and cried in that, to her, almost forgotten tongue: "Oh, who are you? Are you not Ma-to-to'-pa's daughter?"

"Yes! Yes! And you — who are you that speaks to me in my own language?"

"I? Why, I am Crow Woman! Your Arickaree friend in the long ago," she cried. And at that the two embraced and wept tears of joy.

A little later, when Crow Woman had told her her story, Mrs. Kipp asked her if she was contented with her lot.

"I have no children of my own," she replied, "but I love my almost-daughter, the daughter of a dead wife of Lone Otter. I have raised the child. I love her as though she were my very own. But for her, I would long ago have again tried to escape and return to my people."

"Your relatives and mine, too, are all dead. But you shall be free. Before the setting of this sun, you shall be free, and you shall remain with me so long as we live!" Mrs. Kipp cried. She went at once to Lone Otter and bargained with him, paying him a fabulous price — thirty horses, a gun, ten blankets and much tobacco — for Crow Woman and his daughter that she loved.

Would that I could have been present at the meeting of those long parted friends! Their life together and their love for their adopted daughter were ideal. After the buffalo were exterminated and we settled down at Fort Conrad, the old women and the girl planted a garden by the river each season and laboriously watered the hills of corn, beans and squash with buckets which they carried up the steep bank. Beside the garden they built a shelter of boughs to protect them from the sun and from which to watch their growing crops. Thither I went on hot afternoons to sit with them and listen to their tales of the long ago. While they talked, they did wonderfully beautiful colored porcupine quill embroidery work on buffalo leather and buffalo robes that remained to us after our trade had vanished. One piece of work that they undertook required two summers to complete! It was a huge sun, embroidered in all the colors of the rainbow on the flesh side of a fine head and tail buffalo cow robe!

Here to this garden shelter by the river also came Hugh Monroe, or Mah-kwi'-i-pwo-ahts, Rising Wolf, to exchange reminiscences with his oldtime women friends. As I sat and listened to them, I thanked my stars that I was there and that I understood the Blackfeet language as well as they did. Monroe could not speak Mandan nor Arickaree; they could not understand English. The Blackfeet was the language common to us all.

Hugh Monroe, or Rising Wolf, as he was best known, was the son of Captain Hugh Monroe of the English army and Amelie Monroe, a daughter of the De la Roche family, French emigres in Canada. He was born in Three Rivers, Quebec, July 9, 1798, and on May 3, 1814, was apprenticed to the Hudson's Bay Company. In the following spring he arrived at the Company's post, Mountain Fort, on Bow River, the main fork of the South Saskatchewan River. He was immediately detailed to live with the Pi-kun'-i, the so-called Piegan tribe of the Blackfeet confederacy, and a few days later went south with it for the winter. He was the first white man to see the great plains and mountains that lie between the upper reaches of the Saskatchewan and Missouri Rivers. He soon married a daughter of Lone Walker, head chief of the tribe, by whom he had a fine family of stalwart sons and daughters. Not long after his marriage, he severed his connections with the Hudson's Bay Company, became a "free trapper," and lived most of the time with his chosen people, the Pi-kun'-i, to the time of his death in 1896. He was a man of high character and was loved by all who knew him.

Earth Woman, Crow Woman and Rising Wolf, what changes they witnessed as they grew from youth to old age! They saw the beginning of the great fur trade in the Northwest and its end with the extinction of the buffalo and the near extermination of the beaver. They saw the keel boats and the bateaux of the early traders give way to powerful "fire boats" on the Saskatchewan and Missouri and these in turn superseded by railways that brought hordes of settlers to the broad plains!

Perhaps the crowning event of their long lives was a trip by rail to Great Falls after it had become a city. There we talked over a telephone, and they marveled! In the evening I gave them a ride on the electric cars and finally took them to the power house. There they saw red-blue-green flashes of electricity playing about the dynamoes and were completely overcome with astonishment.

"I am sick, heartsick!" Earth Woman exclaimed after we had gone out. "All my life I have prayed to the gods as my father and mother taught me to do. And now this night I have seen with my own eyes that white men, not Thunder Bird, are makers of the lightning. Perhaps there is no Thunder Bird! Perhaps there are no gods! The sun himself, maybe he is nothing but a ball of fire, by white men set rolling across the sky to make the days!"

"Hush! sister, hush!" Crow Woman told her. "Doubt not! What if the white men do make lightning? That has nothing to do with us — with our beliefs! Our ancient ones *saw* Thunder Bird! — heard him thunder as he arose in flight, saw his lightning flashes. Thunder Bird lives! So do all our gods! Take courage! Keep strong your faith in them!

The next morning Earth Woman was herself again. She had prayed to the gods, made sacrifices to them, and her doubts and fears had vanished. After breakfast we all stood upon an upper piazza of the hotel and looked down upon the city and the nearby river. Crow Woman pointed across it to the mouth of Sun River and said, "Just above the place where the two rivers join, just a little way up the smaller stream, is where the Kai'-na captured me!"

"Ai!" said Rising Wolf. "And here, just about where this sleeping and eating house stands, I once saved Jim Bridger and his band of trappers from being attacked and killed by a war party of five hundred North Blackfeet! I often ran buffalo where are now all these houses!"

"Right out there to the still water just above the falls came Sacagawea with the first Long Knives," said Earth Woman. "For days and days, so she told me, they rolled their boats on long wheels up the long trail from below the lower falls to this point and, launching them, went on up the river. I know how the Snake woman felt, how anxious she was to go on, hoping that at the head of the river or on the other slope of the mountains she would meet her people. Day and night she prayed the gods, made sacrifices to them, to guide her to her people!"

"Ai! She did meet them! And induced them to be friends with the Long Knives!" Rising Wolf exclaimed. "But for her there would have been a gathering of the Snake tribes to kill off the white men, and they would have been killed, every one of them. I know! But I have told you the story of it as the Snake chief told it to me in the long ago."

Well, they are gone, Rising Wolf, Earth Woman, Crow Woman and a host of other friends in the old buffalo days! Did they find the Shadow Land, I wonder, and their shadow people living in shadow lodges and on shadow horses running shadow buffalo?

Glad I am that I knew them, gentle, honest, generous friends that they were! Glad I am that through them I am able to add something to our knowledge of Sacagawea and Lewis and Clark and their men.

Chapter II

Rising Wolf and the Snake Chief

Now, to turn on the light, let us begin with Rising Wolf's story of Bird Woman, Sacagawea:

In the summer of 1816, my second year on the plains, I , Rising Wolf, again went south from Mountain Fort with the Pi-kun'-i. We moved leisurely from stream to stream along the foot of the Rockies trapping beavers, and winter struck us while we were camped on Sun River.

After about a foot of snow had fallen and there was little danger of war parties being abroad, my almost-brother, Red Crow, and I obtained permission from his father, Chief Lone Walker, to go south to Deep Creek on a trapping expedition. One of the chief's wives, Rattle Woman, and his daughter, Mink Woman, a girl of about fourteen winters, went with us to keep our lodge in shape and to flesh and dry the skins of the beavers that we should catch.

We made camp on the creek at the foot of the mountains and were there surprised by a number of Snake Indians suddenly entering our lodge. They came, they said, from the camp of their people on the next stream to the west. They knew that we were Blackfeet, and their chief, Black Lance, begged us to take pity upon him and his children. They were all very poor, very hungry. Would we not aid them in making peace with the Blackfeet and in obtaining permission for them to remain on the Blackfeet plains during the winter and kill what Blackfeet buffalo they needed?

We agreed to do what they asked, and the next day Red Crow went with the peace messengers to his father. A council was held and peace was made between the two tribes. It was agreed that the Snakes should camp beside the Pi-kun'-i and kill all the game that they needed. They were not, however, to trap beavers or other fur animals.

Peace declared, I became quite friendly with Black Lance, the Snake chief. I was anxious to learn if there were any opposition traders in his country. So on the first evening that I visited him, the evening following the departure of his peace messengers and Red Crow for the camp on Sun River, I signed to him: "You say that you are friendly to white men. Tell me about those that you know and where they camp." All our talk was in the sign language.

"We know but few," he answered. "Far to the south, we have met a few white men that are not white [Spaniards]. They are almost as red-skinned as we are and their hair is black. They have many horses and mules, plenty of guns, plenty of long sharp-pointed lances. They wear shirts of woven iron which no arrows nor lances will pierce. They will not sell us guns, and so we raid their herds and take their guns whenever that is possible. But we are poor. In our whole tribe there are only twenty guns, and they are useless, as we have no food for them.

"We know a few real white men: two chiefs, Long Knife and Red Hair, and their thirty followers, one of whom is a black white man. I do not lie to you. Truly, his skin is as black as a coal, and his short hair is black and curls tightly to his head! Strange are the ways of the gods! They caused one of our women, a woman we had given up for dead, to bring these white men to us. I must tell you about it."

Here the chief made the sign for a name: the fingers of the right hand tightly closed, thumb extended and placed against the forehead; the hand then raised upward and outward with a graceful sweep. He then made the sign for grass: right hand held out, palm up, fingers and thumb separated and turned up, and then the hand moved from left to right in front of the body. Next he made the sign for woman: fingers of both hands touching on top of the head, and then the hands parting and moving downward on each side of the head, meaning parted hair. What he signed then was "Name, Grass Woman." As he made the signs, he said orally three times, "Bo-i'-naiv! Bo-i'-naiv! Bo-i'-naiv!" Then he signed on, "Did you ever hear of her?"

"No! I know nothing about her," I answered. But right then I knew that the white men were Lewis and Clark and their men. I was to learn all about them and how a Snake woman named Grass Woman [Sacagawea] had brought them to her people. I was more than impatient for him to begin the story. He expressed great surprise that I had never heard of her and then went on—

"Yes, that was her name, Grass Woman. Later we called her Lost Woman and still later, after the great happening, we named her Water-White-Men Woman." He paused thoughtfully for a moment or two and continued. "I will both make the signs for the three names and speak them. Repeat them after me."

In signs: "Grass Woman." Orally: "Bo-i'-naiv."

In signs: "Lost Woman." Orally: "Wad-zi-wip'."

In signs: "Water-White-Men Woman." Orally: "Bah-rai'-bo!"

Over and over I repeated the words after him. "Bo-i'-naiv! Wad-zi-wip'! Bah-rai'-bo!" Then I signed again: "No, I have never heard of her."

"You shall know all!" Black Lance signed.

He thus began his story about Grass Woman:

"It was twenty winters back. We were camped in our own country on the other side of the mountains. Elk and deer became few and we began to starve; we grew very thin. Summer came and still we starved, so our chiefs decided that we must go out upon the buffalo plains of the Blackfeet or die where we were from hunger. We should probably, they said, be killed off by the Blackfeet, but it was better to die with a full belly and quickly than to die slowly from want of food.

"We packed up and crossed the summit of the great mountains, descended the North Fork [Jefferson River] of the Big-River-of-the-Plains [Missouri River], and made camp just above its junction with two other forks [Gallatin and Madison Rivers]. There we came upon some buffalo, killed a number of them and feasted.

"Three mornings later, when most of our men were scattered out on the hunt, a large war party was discovered coming up the valley. The women and children and what few men there were in camp fled. Many of them scattered out in the brush, hid themselves and were not discovered. Others, crazed with fear, ran on and on up the trail in the valley. The enemy pursuing them killed four men, four women and seven youths and captured four boys and five girls. Then, rounding up a large herd of our horses, they rode off down the valley. In time, all the boys and all but two girls escaped from their captors, and then we learned that the enemy had not been Blackfeet as we thought but had come from one of the villages near the Earth House people [Mandans]. They live far down in the valley of the Big-River-of-the-Plains at the eastern edge of the country of the Blackfeet.

"Our people mourned a long time for their dead. The mother of Grass Woman, one of the girls who were captured and did not return, lost also her man in the fight. There remained to her two sons and one daughter, but the mother grieved for the lost man and daughter and soon died from mourning for them.

"The summers came and went. War parties of Blackfeet and of the Earth House people often came into our country, fought us and ran off herds of our horses. We were always hungry in our country; often we starved there. When we could, when winters came and we were not likely to be discovered, we would come out here where we are now and hunt buffalo and live well.

"It was twelve summers back that the sky gods became angry and allowed no rain to fall upon our country, not even one rain. We prayed to them, made sacrifices to them, but still they withheld the rain. So it was that the berry bushes were barren that summer, and the dry earth produced but a few small roots. There was no grass for our horses except in a few damp places. Came winter again, and what few deer and elk there were, left our country. We could not tell what way they went. We moved south, found a few bands of them and during the winter killed them all. When summer came again we were very weak, and some of the weakest were dying from starvation.

"With the first sprouting of the new grass, we moved slowly northward and then to the pass at the head of the North Fork of the Big-River-of-the-Plains. We found no buffalo there, only a few elk and deer, and they were very wild. With only bows and arrows, we could kill but few of them.

We lived mostly upon roots and kept looking out toward the plains, well knowing that they were covered with buffalo, but because of the Blackfeet, we were afraid to venture out there. We remained where we were, hoping that in time the buffalo would come up the North Fork.

"Day after day while we camped there, we kept a man on the trail in the valley of the North Fork watching for the enemy and for the hoped for coming of the buffalo. One morning this watcher discovered men approaching on foot. They were strangely dressed. From their appearance he believed them to be white men. From tribes to the west of us we had learned that there were white skinned men. They had come in big boats on the Everywhere-Salt-Water [Pacific Ocean] to the mouth of our Big River [Columbia River] and had there traded goods, even a few guns, to the tribes who go about in log canoes and who live upon fish.

"The watcher saw that one white man was on the trail and that away off to each side of him three others skulked along in the brush. The one on the trail waved to him and made peace signs. The watcher sat on his horse and allowed the white man to come quite near, near enough for him to see that he really was a white man. But all the time the others were sneaking on through the brush as though with intent to capture him. Fear overcame him. He turned his horse and fled up the valley, called his family together and led them off up a branch stream, there to hide until the white men should have disappeared. He did not come over the pass to us as he should have done.

"Two days later down on our side of the pass, one of our men and his women, out digging roots, discovered the four white men and hurried to our camp with the news. The white men kept on down the trail and suddenly came upon two women and a girl digging roots. The young woman fled from them. The two others could not run; they just sat where they were, expecting to be struck on the head and killed. But no! The lead white man [Captain Lewis] came up to them, took the old woman by the hands, raised her to her feet and signed to her that he was of white skin and meant her no harm. He at once gave her presents, wonderful presents the like of which had never been seen by our people.

Most wonderful of all was a flat, smooth square of ice-rock in which she could see her face. She looked into it, saw her old, wrinkled cheeks, her sunken eyes, the worn down teeth in her jaws, and sank to the ground in horror of herself. Again the white man raised her up, gave her other presents, beads, awls and paint, and she forgot her fears and called to the young woman to return. When the young woman came, the white man gave her presents too and then painted the cheeks of the women and the girl with bright red paint. One of the men with this chief was half white, half Indian, and a good sign talker. He signed to the women and asked them to lead the way to their camp. They signed back that they would do so and started off down the trail.

"Now, when the man digging roots with his women had discovered the four strangers, he had ridden as fast as he could down to our camp and cried out that enemies were coming. We at once mounted our horses and, following our chief, Black Bow, hurried up the trail to meet them and kill them. But what was our surprise, as we neared them, to see that they were different from our enemies of the plains. They wore different clothing. One of them carried a beautiful red, white and blue peace-waver tied to a long stick. We rode still closer to them and saw that their skins were white. Our women with them cried out that they were good men and held up before us the presents they had received. We all dismounted and, after our chief, in turn embraced the white men. We then gathered in a circle, took off our moccasins and smoked and talked with the newcomers in the sign language. They explained that they had come from far east, that their great white chief had sent them to find a trail through the mountains to the shore of the Everywhere-Salt-Water, to make peace with all the tribes along the way and to get them to make peace with one another.

"After three pipes were smoked, the white chief, Long Knife, gave us presents. He also handed Black Bow the peace-waver and said that, as the day was hot and there was no water where we were, he would like us to take him and his men to our camp. We at once sent some young men ahead to fix up for them the one real lodge that we had and then took the trail with the strangers. We arrived in camp some time before sunset, and Black Bow took the strangers to the lodge and told them that it was their lodge.

"After they had rested for a time, we held another council with them, and they then told us that more of their kind were coming up the Big-River-of-the-Plains in boats, and that with them was a woman of our tribe who had long ago been captured by our enemy, the Earth House people. They asked that we take plenty of horses and go to meet the party and pack their property to our camp.

"'It is a forked tongue that this white chief has,' said one of our old warriors. 'I doubt not that there are white men in boats across there on the river, but something tells me that there are with them a multitude of our plains enemies. If we do as we are asked, we go straight to our death!'

"At once there was much talk in that council lodge. Some of the warriors agreed with the old man that the white men were trying to draw them into a trap. Said another warrior: 'If all is just as these white men say, then they are after all but a small party. They are rich in the things that we most need, guns and powder and balls, with which to defend ourselves from the attacks of our plains enemies. I propose that we at once send messengers to the other tribes of our Snake Nation and to our friends, the Flatheads, and ask them to come and help us wipe out these white men and take their property.'

"'Yes! Yes! That is what we should do! Let us send the messengers at once!' cried one man after another until nearly all had spoken. Then said our chief, Black Bow, 'You speak wisely. If we can take all the white men's guns, with the great quantity of powder and ball that they surely have, we can go out on the plains, hold our own against our enemies and get all the buffalo that we want. Let the messengers go at once for help. And to hasten matters, let us do what the white men ask. We will take horses and bring their men and their property up here. We shall then have them right here in our camp, where we can take them unaware and easily kill them. Now, who will furnish horses and go with the white men and me tomorrow?'

"Many of the warriors answered that they would take extra horses and go with him, but during the night a great fear came upon most of them, fear that they were to be led into a trap, that back of the whites were hundreds of their plains enemies, either Blackfeet or Earth House people or both. In the morning when the time came to leave, but eight men started out with our chief and the white men. I, Black Lance, was one of the eight. We had not traveled far, however, when we were overtaken by many of the afraid ones, some of them accompanied by their women. After we left the camp, Black Bow's woman had grieved for him and then, crying out that she was not a coward, that she was braver than the men, had caught a horse and made ready to follow our trail. Because she shamed them, the best of the men and women hurried to catch up their horses and take the trail with her.

"On that first day out we crossed over the pass in the mountains and made camp by some springs high up on the east slope of the mountains. On the next morning, as soon as we were ready to go on, the white man chief sent two of his men ahead, saying that they were to hunt, and asked us to keep with him so that the game would not become alarmed. This alarmed us. We thought that the two men were being sent to tell the enemy to be ready to spring upon us. Many of our people turned back right there, and we who went on sent several of our men forward on each side of the valley to keep watch of the two white hunters. They really were hunters. During the day, they killed some deer and gave us most of the meat. When evening came, we were thinking that perhaps the white men meant us no harm and that everything was just as they had said.

"On the next morning we arose very early, and the white chief at once sent one of his men and one of us with him to look for the white men who were coming up the river in boats. I went off by myself, keeping close to the river, and soon saw the white men, all of them working hard to drag and push their boats up the swift water. I ran back to camp, crying out that I had seen the whites. Then we all hurried on to meet them. By that time they had come quite close to our camp. Two of the whites were on the shore ahead of the boats, and with them was a woman. One of our women ran forward. Other women followed her, and when we saw them embrace the lone woman, we knew that it was as the white chief had told us, that there was one of our women in his party. Right there we lost all of our fears. Had there been plains enemies with the whites, this woman would have so signed to us as soon as we came in sight. The two white men came on. One of them was the other chief of the party, he whom we named Red Hair [Captain Clark]. Our chief, Black Bow, embraced him and so did the rest of us, and then we led the two white chiefs to one of our brush shelters for a council. We took off our moccasins, the pipe was lighted, and the white chiefs told one of their men to bring the Snake woman to interpret for us.

"She came, this young woman, with her little child in her arms, came with downcast eyes, with hesitating steps, and timidly sat just without our half circle. I looked at her, so did the others, and none of us recognized her. Black Bow at once opened the council. 'Woman,' said he, 'interpret these my words: White men chiefs, we are glad that you are coming to our country.'

"As he said that, the woman for the first time looked up at him, and then, leaving her child, she sprang across the circle and embraced him. Laughing and crying at the same time, trembling as though from the cold, she arose and placed her blanket across his shoulders, then again knelt beside him and cried, 'Oh, brother! Do you not know me? I am your sister, Grass Woman!'

"'So you are! So you are!' Black Bow exclaimed and in turn embraced her.

"Some of us cried out, 'She is Grass Woman! Our *Lost Woman*! She has returned to us!'

"Then, trembling and trying to dry her eyes, she asked her brother to give her news of relatives. He answered, 'Our father was killed by the enemies that took you.'

"'Yes, I know,' Grass Woman said. 'As the enemy bore me away, I saw our father's body lying beside the trail!'

"'Grieving for our father and for you, our mother soon died. Then our sister died, then our brother, Middle Sun. Of all our family there remain only our brother, Little Otter, whom I have sent with a message to our Snake peoples, and our little nephew, son of our sister, Deer Robe.

"Now, when Grass Woman heard that, she broke out crying again. Sitting there with her arms on her brother's shoulder, she wept bitterly. But suddenly one of the white men spoke to her angrily. 'It is my man,' she said. 'He orders me back to my place to interpret. Badly as I feel, I must obey him.' And she returned to her child. But try as she would, she could not stop crying, so the council was put off until later in the day.

"Came now the rest of the white men with their boats and made camp. We watched them and near went crazy with wonder at them and the strange and useful things that they had! One of those white men was black. We could not believe that his skin was not covered with a shining black paint, until one of us washed his forearm, scrubbing and scrubbing it without result. We were struck with the number of different shaped kettles and other utensils in which the white men cooked their food. We marveled at the number of fine long guns they carried and, oh, how we wanted to see what was in the many bundles that they carried from the boats to their camp! They had sharp, heavy, wood-handled pieces of shiny hard rock with which they cut wood. With but a few blows of one of them, they cut down good size trees. That was great medicine!

"While the white men fixed up their camp, Black Bow talked with his sister, and we sat by them and listened. She told about her life with our enemies and of her marriage to the white man. But what most interested us was what she said about the riches of her captors and the ease in which they lived. Their homes were large earth-covered lodges, which the severest cold of winter could not penetrate. Near their lodges they raised each summer great quantities of good food plants, which they dried for winter use. Their plains were always covered with buffalo and antelope. The timbered valley of their Big River was full of elk and deer. They knew not what it was to hunger or suffer from cold.

"'Neither should we suffer from hunger and cold nor fear our enemies if we had guns!' the chief cried out. 'Well, we shall have guns! Little sister, when our brother and the other messengers return, bringing with them the warriors of our Snake tribes to help us, we shall kill these white men and take their guns and their great store of powder and ball and then go out and live on the buffalo plains!'

"Grass Woman gave a cry of distress and shrank away from him. 'You are crazy even to think of doing that,' she told him. 'What if you do take them unaware while they sleep and kill them off? Of what use would the guns be that you would get, thirty or forty of them, against the two hundred and more guns of the Earth House people? Brother, you must do all that you can for these white men, for they are men of great heart and your true friends. Have they not told you why they have come into this country, that they are here to get all tribes to make peace with one another? Have they not told you that they come to make a trail for white traders to follow, so that you may all have guns and traps and other things that you need to make yourselves rich and comfortable?'

"'Yes, they said all that to us, but we did not believe them,' Black Bow answered.

"'Then believe it now! I, your true sister, tell you it is so!'

"'Truly, my mind is all in a whirl. I must think about this!' the chief exclaimed.

"By this time the white men had set up their camp, and they now invited us to it to counsel with them. We were seated under a shelter of cloth and willows where we took off our moccasins and smoked by turns one pipe. The white chief named Long Knife then spoke to us, Grass Woman's man telling her what he said, and she in turn interpreting the words to us. He told us that his great white chief had sent him and his men to make friends with all tribes all the way to the Everywhere-Salt-Water and to get them to make peace with one another. He hoped that we would make peace with the tribes with whom we were at war, for that would please the great white chief, and he would send men with guns, traps and all kinds of goods to trade to us, and ever afterward we should have plenty of everything, food, clothing, warm lodges, tobacco, and we could roam where we pleased without fear of attack. Now he asked us to help him: he wanted horses, plenty of our horses for riding and packing on his way westward from our country, and he would pay us well for them.

"Then said Black Bow to Grass Woman, 'Sister, had you not told me that these men are of straight tongue and good heart, I should not have believed anything that they told us. I now do believe. I am sure it is all as you say, that they mean only good for us. You may tell them that we will furnish them horses, that we shall do all that we can for them, and that we hope their traders will soon come to us with plenty of guns, traps, and goods of all kinds.'

"'Brother, you really mean that — is it straight from your heart?' Grass Woman asked.

"'It is!' he answered.

"'Then send other messengers at once to our Snake people and the Flatheads to tell them to remain where they are, for the white men are their friends and are to travel safely through our country,' she demanded.

"'They shall start this day,' he agreed.

"At that she embraced him and, through her man, told the whites that the chief said that all should be as they wished and that he hoped traders would come to them as soon as possible. Thereupon the council ended, and the white chiefs gave us valuable and beautiful presents. Black Bow was given a beautiful suit of white chief clothes and a medal. We all received shirts, leggings, knives, tobacco, medals, looking glasses and awls. Last we were feasted with big dishes of a boiled plant that our Grass Woman told us had been raised by her Earth House people captors. Next to good meat, it was the best food we had ever eaten.

"We had not enough horses to move all the property of the white men, so we took Red Hair and some of his men and Grass woman across the pass to our main camp and then sent some of our young men with plenty of horses to bring over the rest of the party and all their property.

"Now, before Grass Woman was captured by our plains enemies, she had been given by her father and mother to a man of our tribe named Little Mountain. She was to become his wife when she grew up. Returning now to the camp after a long visit to one of our tribes, he heard that she was there and ran about until he found her. 'Ha! There you are, Grass Woman, Lost Woman!' he cried. 'You have grown up, I see. You look strong and you are handsome.

Well, I am glad of it because I need you. Get whatever things you have and come over with me to my shelter.'

"'I shall not go with you! You are nothing to me!' Grass Woman told him.

"'You are my woman! You shall go with me! I gave your father three horses, and he promised that I should have you as soon as you became a woman,' he insisted.

"'I will prove to you that I am not your woman,' she told him and, throwing open her blanket, she held up to his view her child. 'See. This is my boy, and that white man there is my man and the father.'

"'Ha! That makes it different! I do not want you!' Little Mountain told her and turned and went his way.

At this point, Black Lance halted the telling of his story. "As Black Bow had promised his sister we should do, that we did for the Long Knives," concluded Black Lance. "We furnished them the horses that they needed and a man to guide them through our country, and they went on their way toward the Everywhere-Salt-Water. We heard afterward that they had great difficulty in passing through the mountains, that they could find no game and would have starved to death had they not killed and eaten some of the horses that we gave them. Well, they made their way to the shore of the Great Water and there wintered and in the following summer returned and went on eastward. We have not heard of them again. Summer after summer we have looked for the white traders that they promised to send to us with plenty of guns for us to buy, but the summers pass and they do not come. Tell me, white youth, do you think that they ever will come?"

"I cannot answer that," I told him. "I, Rising Wolf, have no knowledge of the Long Knife traders. Myself, I am a Red Coat trader. At our post in the north, we have plenty of guns, traps, all kinds of things to trade to you if you go there with your furs."

Black Lance made a gesture of despair. "That we can never do," he signed. "The Blackfeet tribes will never permit us to do that! If they now allow us to camp out here until green grass time and kill a few of their buffalo, it will be more than we ever expected of them. Summer will soon come again and back we must go across the mountains, there in hunger to hide from the war parties of Blackfeet, Earth House people, Assiniboines, Crees, who come to kill us and take our horses. White youth, we Snakes are a poor and most unhappy people!" signed Black Lance

Well, what answer could I make except to sign to him that he must take courage? My heart went out to him and his harried people, but I could do nothing. I knew even better than he that the Blackfeet never would give the Snakes an opportunity to trade for guns if they could prevent it.

Chapter III

Rising Wolf Starts on His Mission
and Meets Bird Woman

Rising Wolf continues his story:

Upon leaving the north with the Pi-kun'-i, our factor, Terrible Tongue, as the Blackfeet called Hardesty, had charged me to do everything in my power to bring about peace between the Pi-kun'-i and the Cheyennes and to induce the latter to come north with us in the spring and trade at Mountain Fort.

This was no small task that had been imposed upon me. The Blackfeet tribes had ever been at war with the Cheyennes, who were themselves a powerful plains people, great trappers and tanners of robes and owners of large herds of horses. Indeed, the Blackfeet name for them was Spotted Horses people, on account of the strain of pinto horses that they particularly bred and which the Blackfeet raided at every opportunity. Naturally the Blackfeet and particularly the Pi-kun'-i, southernmost of the tribes, did not wish to make peace with a people from whom they took the beautiful pinto animals. They were foes worth keeping as foes.

As I expected when I mentioned the matter to Lone Walker, he told me at once that there could be no thought of peace with the Cheyennes. This much I knew about them: they roamed the plains south and east of the Yellowstone, and traded their furs and robes to the Earth House tribes, who lived in fortified villages on the Missouri below the mouth of the Yellowstone. With these tribes the Blackfeet had ever been upon friendly terms, and Lone Walker had some especially close friends in the chiefs of the Earth House people, the Mandans.

As a way of getting in touch with the Cheyennes, Red Crow and I began importuning Lone Walker to allow us to visit the Mandans. At first he laughed at our request, but we kept at him about it, and he finally agreed that we might go if we could find some of his proved warriors to accompany us and could take with us some presents for his friends. The camp crier was accordingly told to make the round of the lodges and call for volunteers to go with us, but we got no response and were in despair when, several evenings later, a man named Heavy Robe and nicknamed Never Talks came into our lodge and told Lone Walker that he would go with us to the Earth House tribes. Red Crow and I could hardly believe our ears. That Heavy Robe, of all men, should propose to take us on the long trail was almost too good for belief.

"I am glad that you will go with my boys," Lone Walker told him. "I wanted three or four men, but you are as good as four. When will you be ready to start?"

"Whenever you give the word."

"Then leave day after tomorrow," the chief decided.

Heavy Robe arose, wrapped his robe about him and said, shortly, "I shall be ready at that time," and went out with never a word to Red Crow and me.

Now you may think that this has nothing to do with Sacagawea. But wait!

We got an early start on the appointed morning and made quite a cavalcade as we set out, for we each took an extra saddle horse and with them four fine horses and a pack load of goods, which Lone Walker and his under chiefs were sending with many messages of peace and good will to the chiefs of the tribes we were to visit.

It was a long, long way that we had to go to reach the villages below the mouth of the Yellowstone. We struck the Musselshell River, followed it down to the Missouri and then followed the windings of its deep and timbered valley, for the snow was too deep for traveling upon the plains. Below the mouth of the Musselshell, it became so deep that we could not travel at all except in the winding, hard-beaten trails of the buffalo and other game.

Day after day we went on and on, ever in sight of countless herds of game but finding no enemies to bar our way.

We said nothing to our leader about our desire to meet with Cheyennes and induce them to make peace with our people. The time had not come for that nor did we have the slightest idea how we could meet them. "Just trust in the gods; they will show us the way!" Red Crow kept telling me.

All went well with us until one evening several days after we had passed the mouth of the Yellowstone. We were about to make camp when a bitterly cold, suddenly rising north wind brought to us the strong odor of cottonwood smoke. "Ha! We must be near the Earth House people!" I said.

Heavy Robe looked back at me and motioned me to be silent. Then after looking ahead for some time, he said to us, "If this smoke were coming from a village, we should hear the sounds of it, people talking, children shouting — anyhow, the barking of dogs. The odor of the smoke is strong. It is coming from a fire in this grove of timber. Either enemies are close ahead of us or a party of hunters from the Earth House villages!"

"What shall we do?" Red Crow asked.

"There is but one thing to do," our leader answered. "We will go on. It may be that we can circle around the camp without being seen. We will try to do so. Look to the priming of your guns! Be watchful!"

With that he led on, branching out from trail to trail away from the river. The wind with its odor of smoke came to us in eddying swirls, sometimes in our faces, sometimes on our right or left. We could not determine from it just where the fire was, but we believed it to be in the lower part of the grove and near the river.

On this day I was in the rear with four horses between me and Red Crow, who was driving the rest of the loose stock after Heavy Robe. We had not gone more than a couple of hundred yards when suddenly I heard something plunk into the lower flap of my robe in front of my left thigh. My horse made a sudden leap that threw me back upon him behind the saddle. I should have gone clear off had I not been pinned to the horse: an arrow in my robe and into his wither pinned me to him. As I jounced back into the saddle with a yell, I looked around and saw a man in a side trail not fifty yards away. He was fitting a fresh arrow to his bow, and farther out in the grove a dozen men were coming on the run on his trail, holding their weapons ready to attack us. As

I fired at the first man and he fell, one of the others, the only one of them who had a gun, fired and shot down the horse directly in front of me. At that my horse flinched back and I had no little difficulty in making him leap the obstruction. I passed it just as Red Crow and Heavy Robe fired. Out of the corner of my eye, I saw another one of the enemy go down. We drew away from them as fast as we could go, their arrows dropping harmlessly behind us.

The snow was so deep that the enemy could not come directly after us from the side trail they were in. They had to follow it up to its junction with our trail and then turn down the main trail. We soon passed out of sight of them. Nevertheless, they kept after us, yelling all the time. By that we knew that the rest of their party were somewhere ahead of us, gathered around the fire from which came the smoke, now stronger than ever in our nostrils.

We had no more than finished loading when we saw forty or fifty men ahead, in our trail, running toward us. Between them and us was no branch trail. Noting that, Heavy Robe called out that we must turn back and take a branch trail we had just passed. I turned my horse at once and so became the leader. It was no easy task for Red Crow and Heavy Robe to turn the loose animals about to follow me. We lost time, and a cloud of arrows and one gunshot were discharged at us by the lower enemy party while we were making the turnabout.

As soon as Heavy Robe had his part of the loose stock turned and following Red Crow, he stopped his animal and fired back and killed the lead man of the enemy. He then came on, hurrying to overtake us.

I now came to the trail branching from ours obliquely down the valley and toward the river. I passed the trail, turned my horse square about, hoping thereby to force the loose animals to turn into it. They did not understand what was wanted of them and came to a halt, and Red Crow was obliged to flounder his horse past them and ride into the trail. Then Heavy Robe urged the horses on, and as they could not pass me, they were obliged to turn into the branch and follow Red Crow. All that took valuable time, during which both parties of the enemy were closing in upon us.

Heavy Robe's gun was empty, but Red Crow and I fired our pieces, he at the lower and I at the upper party, and we each wounded a man, how seriously we could not tell. Their comrades passed them and ran after us, firing their two guns and their arrows at long range, again without effect, and we soon rode out of sight of them.

On and on we went through grove after grove of timber and through open bottoms. We were tired, we were hungry, but we dared not stop. Heavy Robe said that we must keep going until midnight, and we would then halt only long enough to cook and eat some meat. I kept my eyes upon the Seven Persons, the big dipper, and thought that they never had swung around so slowly. Then when they pointed to a little more than midnight time, we rode into a trail in the timber and saw on both sides of it the snow strewn with small tree cuttings and shreds of bark. Heavy Robe called back to us, "This is the work of the Earth House people. You shall soon see their village!" That was good news.

We went on faster in the broad, hard-beaten trail. Soon we emerged from the grove and saw out ahead in the long, wide bottom a dark splotch in its whiteness, which Heavy Robe said was the upper village of the Pi-nap'-ut-se-na, or Lower Gros Ventres, otherwise called the Minnetarees. "There they are, our friends!" he said. "We shall be welcome there — yes, more than welcome when we tell them that we have certainly killed three Assiniboines and wounded two more right here in the Minnetarees' Big River Valley!"

As we neared the village, we saw that it was surrounded by a stockade of cottonwood posts. The trail led us to a passageway, which had been closed for the night with an inset of heavy posts. We came to a halt before it, and Heavy Robe shouted, "Open, friends! Open the way for us!"

Three or four times he shouted. Then we heard footsteps creaking upon hard frozen snow, and finally four or five men looked down upon us from the top of the stockade, and one of them spoke. Of course we could not understand his language nor he our tongue, but when he spoke he also used the sign language, in which he asked us who we were.

"We are your friends! We are Pi-kun'-i!" Heavy Robe signed in answer. At once the passageway was cleared for us. As we rode in and dismounted, the men embraced us and signed to us that we were welcome in their village.

People were now coming to us from all parts of it. One of them, a robe wrapped man who thrust his face almost into mine, gave me quite a shock of surprise by saying to me in French, "You are white. Who are you and where are you from?"

"I am Hugh Monroe...Rising Wolf. We come from the camp of the Pi-kun'-i Blackfeet," I answered.

"Ha! You are English. But you speak French as though you were French!" he exclaimed.

"My mother is a De la Roche," I explained.

"Ha! Yes! The De la Roches of Montreal and Three Rivers!" he exclaimed. "I know the family. That is, I saw them often in my youthful days. Myself, I am Toussaint Charbonneau, one-time Nor'wester, now free man. Free! Free! But of course, you have heard of me."

"No, I can't say that I have," I answered.

"Is it possible! Well, then, I must tell you, " he cried. "Me, I am the man who led the American soldiers Lewis and Clark and their men from here to the Western Ocean and back."

"I have heard of them," I said, "and of a Snake named Grass Woman, who brought them to her people.

"Ha! My woman! Tsaka'-kawia, Bird Woman, as these Minnetarees named her." he cried. "But come, M'sieu Monroe. You and your friends, you shall camp with me!"

While Charbonneau and I talked together, Heavy Robe and Red Crow were telling the Minnetarees in the sign language about our fight with the Assiniboines. As the Frenchman led us to his lodge, the whole village was aroused. The warriors were hurrying out to saddle their horses and ride up the valley to attack the enemy. After unpacking our outfit and tethering our animals to some piles of cottonwood browse, we went inside and found ourselves in a wonderfully warm, comfortable lodge all of forty feet in diameter. Along its walls, about six feet in height, were several raised couches with buffalo leather curtains. In the center a small fire was burning, the smoke going out of a square opening in the upslanting post-and-beam and pole roof, heavily covered with earth, as was the insloping split-log-faced circular wall. As we entered, a woman rose from tending the fire and turned toward us. Thinking to give her a pleasant surprise, I said to her, "How! Bo-i'-naiv!" Well, I did surprise her. She started back with a jerk, clapping a hand to her breast, then recovering herself and addressing me in a torrent of Snake words to which I shook my head negatively and then told her in signs that I did not understand the Snake language. I added that a chief of her people named Black Lance, with many lodges of Snakes, was camping and hunting with our tribe, the Pi-kun'-i Blackfeet. Then Charbonneau broke our conversation by crossly ordering her — in French — to hurry and prepare food for us. Right then and there I conceived an intense dislike for him!

"You must excuse me. You called me by my right name. You mentioned my people. I did not think about the food," she said in good French. She turned to set several earthen pots before the fire. She was a handsome woman of about thirty years. Not tall, rather slender, quick and graceful. Her long, braided hair hung down over her back to her knees. She wore a gown of blue trade cloth trimmed across the breast with several rows of elk tushes and belted at the waist.

I now introduced my friends to Charbonneau. He shook hands with them and told me to tell them that they were welcome in his poor lodge. Then he assigned us our places in it, a couch for my almost-brother and me and another for Heavy Robe. Charbonneau drew aside the curtains to them, and we were glad enough to lay aside our weapons and heavy buffalo robe wraps and sit down to rest. In a few moments the woman had warmed the food and set it before us in gray earthen jars of native make. It was good food, corn boiled with meat, and we ate a lot of it. We had no sooner finished eating than we tumbled over on our couches and almost instantly fell asleep.

Near daylight we were awakened by Charbonneau and sat up to find a tall, heavy set, fine appearing warrior in the lodge, no other than Red Shield, head chief of the village. He informed us that messengers had come in from the party that had gone out against the Assiniboines and had brought bad news. It appeared that we had seen only a part of the enemy, for his men had come upon more than two hundred of them and had been driven back with a loss of seven killed. He had sent to the lower villages for reinforcements, but knew that he could not get many, as most of the men were off on a buffalo hunt down the river. He asked us to go with him with our good guns and help fight our common enemy. Of course we could not refuse to do that and soon after daylight were hurrying with the party he led up the valley. At mid-forenoon we came upon the Minnetarees who had gone out from the village in the night. They were halted before a large grove, at the edge of which the trail was barricaded with a long, high pile of brush. Back of the pile the smoke from several fires was rising in the still cold air. "There they are, the Cut-Throats," the leader of the night party told us. "There they are, safe behind their barricade, roasting meat at their fires, comfortable. We are not strong enough to attack them. They surprised us last night and killed seven of our number!"

"We cannot rush that barricade until help comes from the lower villages," Red Shield declared. So we waited there in the terrible cold. Some time after noon the reinforcements came, about two hundred men from the other Minnetaree village and from that of the Ahnahaways, or Black Moccasins, and the two Mandan villages. The leader of the Mandans was no other than Ma-to-to'-pa, or Four Bears, Lone Walker's close friend. He gave us more than hearty greeting and said that we must visit him as soon as possible and stop with him a long time.

We believed the brush of the barricade concealed heavy dead timber and limbs which our horses could not break through, and the snow was so deep that we could not rush our animals past the ends of the barricade and so flank the enemy behind it. We simply had to make an attack on the trail, and it was certain that some, at least of those in the lead, would fall before they could penetrate the barrier. Red Shield took command of the whole party and ordered that those who had no shield should take the rear of the line. That included Heavy Robe and Red Crow and me, but Heavy Robe declared that as he was now at the head of the line with the chiefs, he would remain with them and so, of course, Red Crow vowed that he would stick close to his leader, and I had to declare that I, Rising Wolf, would too.

Red Shield looked back at the long line of us, more than two hundred riders strung out in single file in the trail, and gave the order to charge. Simultaneously the war song of four different tribes was raised, the most tremendous burst of discord that I ever heard. It quite drowned out the sound of the war song of the Pi-kun'-i, which my companions and I were shouting as loudly as we could.

Back of the barrier the smoke of enemy campfires still rose in the frost filled air, but not a man could we see as we approached the wide, high brush pile across the trail. We did not doubt that two hundred Cut-Throats were watching us through its interstices, confident that they could kill so many of our lead men that the rest would turn and flee from them. Nearer and nearer we rode to the obstruction, and still we could not see even one of the enemy. I wanted, oh, so much to see them. It is far easier, let me tell you, to approach seen danger than it is that which is hidden!

There were ten men ahead of me. I saw them one by one burst through the barricade as though it were so much straw, and then with a few jumps my horse carried me through the gap they had made in the brush. I looked along the length of the barrier and then ahead and laughed a choking, foolish kind of laugh. We had been tricked! The Cut-Throats had cleared six large spaces of snow and on the bared ground had carefully constructed fires of mixed dry and green wood that was sure to smoulder and smoke for a day or more, and then they had gone their way. Around each fireplace was a litter of willow cuttings and strands of rawhide rope and two or three broken, oblong circlets of willow switches. The enemy had made snowshoes and then gone up the beaten trail down which my companions and I had come the previous evening. Heavy frost stood like fuzz in their footprints in the snow, proving that they were hours ahead of us, but anyhow we followed and silently enough. The various tribal war songs had come to a sudden end.

Not far above the barricade we came upon the seven Minnetarees that the Cut-Throats had killed. They were all scalped and horribly mutilated. We passed on through the grove, across a long open bottom, through another grove and came to the place where the enemy had put on their snowshoes and struck off due north across the frozen river. On the opposite side a long point ran out from the plain to a small grove and screened by it, they had left the valley and struck out for their camp on Mouse River perhaps, or farther north on the Assiniboine River. Reluctantly, sullenly, the chase was abandoned right there, and we turned back down the trail. Some of the Minnetarees dropped out to bury their dead, others to go on up the trail to take the scalps and weapons of the Cut-Throats that Heavy Robe and Red Crow and I had killed.

When we returned to the village and dismounted in front of Charbonneau's lodge, Bo-i'-naiv, Sacagawea, came out and told us to put our horses in a small roped in enclosure that she had made. Defying the bitter cold, she had made three or four trips to the distant timber with her travois horse and brought in loads of cottonwood browse for the animals and fuel for the lodge.

"You are very good to us. We must try to do something for you," I told her when we had gone inside and were gathered about the fire.

"I like to do things for real people!" she exclaimed. "I would have done anything — I would have died for Red Hair and Long Knife, the great white chiefs with whom I went to the Western Ocean. Oh, that I could meet them once more, just once before I die."

"Woman! Cease jabbering in your bad French and prepare for us a little dinner!" her man commanded, and she shrank away from him to her work.

Charbonneau had been asleep on his couch when we entered. He now roused up, reached out for his pipe and listlessly asked me what we had accomplished upriver. I answered as shortly as I could that we had been given the slip by the Assiniboines. He laughed.

"I expected something like that would happen," he said. "In one way or another, the Assiniboines generally get the best of these foolish villagers."

"It is not a laughing matter to them that they have lost seven of their number," I somewhat angrily replied.

"Ah, but they should not have gone up there in the night. They might have known they would be ambushed," he sneered.

I had an angry reply ready for that but just then caught Sacagawea's eyes upon me. She signed me not to argue with him, so I turned to my companions and told them what he had said. They made no comment upon it, but I knew from the expression of their faces that they disliked him as much as I did.

"Eat! Eat heartily!" he told us when the woman set food before us. "I am poor, but what I have I share with you so long as it lasts. Yes, I am very poor, M'sieu Monroe. I have only two horses, both small — almost worthless. I have no traps. I am miserable! Now if I had even one good horse, I could do something. I could hunt and set deadfalls for wolves. As I am, I cannot improve my condition."

I turned to my companions. "This man," I told them, "is complaining of his poverty. He is making a talk for one of our horses. As we need him for interpreting, let's give him one."

"Give him my roan horse!" Heavy Robe grimly said. "I would see him dead before he should have anything of mine were it not for this woman. For her sake, give him the horse."

I told Charbonneau at once that we gave him our big roan, and at that he brightened up and became very talkative. Later on, when some chiefs came in to visit with us, I found that we could not use him as an interpreter except in conjunction with his wife. Though he had been with the Minnetarees for years, he had not mastered their language! His way of interpreting was to have Sacagawea tell him in French what the Minnetarees said, and he would then change it into better French or into English. To save time, I had the woman interpret to me in French, and I turned the matter into Blackfeet.

After we had delivered our load of presents to the chiefs with the messages of friendship from Lone Walker, the chiefs went their way. Charbonneau left to gamble in a nearby lodge and left us with Sacagawea. That was just what I wanted. I felt she would help me, and so I said to her, "I want to tell you what is in my heart. My chief, Terrible Tongue, Hudson's Bay Company factor at our Mountain Fort, has ordered me to try to make peace between the Cheyennes and the Blackfeet and persuade the Cheyennes to go north with us in the spring and trade at our post. Tell me how I shall do this."

"Be careful. Don't talk so loudly," she answered, "and if my man comes in, start talking about some other matter."

"You have been good to my Snake people," she went on, "and that is one reason I will help you. Another reason is that I want to help the Cheyennes. Many of them are my friends. They are a brave, clean, hard working people. They trap and hunt all winter and catch great numbers of beaver and tan buffalo robes so soft that they fold like trade cloth. Then in the spring, the Cheyennes come here and get cheated out of the result of their work. If they would only wait for the American traders, they would do well enough. But long before the trade boats come up the river, the Northwesters come from the Assiniboine with packtrains of goods, and they pay the Cheyennes and all who will trade with them almost nothing for their furs. Why, they ask sixty beaver skins for a gun! Twenty skins for a blanket! And for everything else prices beyond reason. Now, your company charges much less, does it not?"

"Only twenty skins for a gun, ten skins for a blanket, and six skins for three yards of trade cloth," I answered.

"Reasonable enough," she said, "and, oh, I do want peace! I would like to see peace among all tribes. I cry when I think of my Snake people. All the tribes of the plains are against them, and they without guns and so unable to defend themselves, hiding and starving for the greater part of the time in the forests of little game on the west side of the mountains.

"Now, listen, Rising Wolf. My man was once a Nor'wester and is still in league with the Nor'westers against all other traders, even the Americans. If he learns that you will try to bring about peace with the Cheyennes in order to get their trade, he will do something to prevent peace. You must tell no one, Minnetaree, Mandan or Ahnahaway that you want their trade. Just say you would like to meet the Cheyennes and bring about a peace between them and the Blackfeet. You remember that chief, Big Man, who was here tonight and to whom you gave presents. He asked you to visit him. Do so, for he is really a Cheyenne adopted by the Mandans and so a chief in both tribes. Try to get him to go with you to the Cheyenne camp. If he will take you there, you will at least be sure to be well received and get a hearing."

"I shall do as you advise," I told her, and we then talked of other things. Sacagawea, Bird Woman, finally wound up the evening by telling me the story of her capture by the Minnetarees.

PART II

BIRD WOMAN'S STORY

Chapter IV

Bird Woman's Story of Her Capture

So here begins Bird Woman — Sacagawea — with her own story as she told it to Rising Wolf — Hugh Monroe:

Bird Woman began — I must first tell you something about my Snake people. It is not because they are cowards that they are poor, that they hide and hunger in the mountain forests. It is because they cannot possibly hold their own against the plains tribes, especially bands of the Blackfeet. Always, when my Snake people went out upon the plains after buffalo, they would be driven back by enemies far outnumbering them. At last, in a summer of little rain when few salmon ascended the rivers, and there were but few roots, the chiefs of the Snakes, the Flatheads, and the Pend'Oreilles held council together.

Said the Snake chief to the others: "It seems to me that we have not had good sense. We have been going out upon the plains to hunt — you Flatheads in one place, you Pend'Oreilles in another, and my people in another. That is where we have made a mistake. Let us now band together and go out to hunt buffalo. We will then number so many warriors that I doubt that the Blackfeet or our other enemies will even attempt to drive us from their plains. Their plains, say I? Why, they are our plains, too, and so are the herds of buffalo and antelope that cover them! Come! Let us make plenty of arrows and then go out and kill all that we want of our plains animals!"

The other chiefs agreed. As soon as they and their warriors had made all the arrows that they could possibly need, the three tribes of them crossed the mountains and camped just above the Great Falls of the Missouri, in the midst of countless herds of buffalo. I do not know how long ago that was — sometime before I was born.

Now the people of the three tribes were happy. They feasted upon the plenty of buffalo that the hunters killed. The women dried great quantities of it for future use and tanned many buffalo hides for warm winter robes and leather for lodge skins. Day after day they kept scouts far out in all directions to watch for the approach of enemies.

At last one morning, enemies were discovered coming from the north. Scouts hurried to camp with the news and said that the enemy party numbered about two hundred men on foot. When the chiefs of the three tribes heard that, they were glad. They laughed. "We are more than six hundred men," they said. "This day we shall teach the enemy something they will never forget! We shall kill all of them except two or three, who shall go home and tell their people that we are now united and so powerful that they cannot drive us from the plains!"

All the warriors of the three tribes mounted their best horses, slung their thick bullhide shields, and with bows and arrows in hand rode out gladly to destroy the enemy war party. There was the enemy, out on the open plain, heading for the valley where the little river meets the big river just above the falls. When they saw our warriors riding out to battle with them, the enemy did not halt. They raised their war song and kept right on. Our chiefs said to one another, "They are crazy! Crazily brave! They should know — but it seems they do not — that we shall soon wipe them out."

Nearer and nearer the Snake, Pend'Oreille and Flathead warriors rode to them, arrows fitted to their bows, and shields held ready to stop the flight of enemy arrows. As our warriors rode, their chiefs cautioned them not to shoot until they were so close to the enemy that they could see their eyes. But before they could ride that near, the enemy came to a halt. Some raised what appeared to be shining sticks and pointed them at our warriors. Suddenly there burst from the ends of the sticks fire and smoke and booms of thunder. Riders and horses fell as though they had been struck by lightning. Five riders and three horses went down. All the rest of the more than six hundred riders turned and fled back to camp and gathered their women and children and what they could of their property, and away they went up the trail to the mountains, once more to hide from their plains enemies and starve in the forests of the west slope.

Never again, they said to one another, could they venture out after buffalo. Their plains enemies had been favored by the gods. They had been given thunder and lightning. It was useless to try to fight enemies who had the weapons of the sky gods, the terrible weapons with which great trees were scattered into splinters, with which even the solid rock of the mountains was broken into small pieces!

There followed winters and summers of hunger for the three tribes. They hid deep in the forests, catching a few salmon, killing a little game, eating what roots they could find. Summer after summer the plains war men sought them, raiding their horse herds and killing many of the people with the thunder and lightning weapons of the sky gods. It was a hard life that those mountain tribes led.

Then at last it was learned that those weapons were not sky god weapons. A party of Snakes, wandering far south, met white men, men who carried these same weapons and said they were not medicine. White men made the weapons themselves and also the black stuff like sand and the round balls with which they fed the weapons. They would not give nor sell the Snakes even one and so, watching for a chance, the war party stole one of the weapons and food for it and hurried north to their people. Thereafter, knowing that these weapons were man-made, not god-made, the Snakes became less timid and at times ventured upon the plains after buffalo, going out generally in the late fall when war parties of the plains tribes had ceased roaming about.

Thus it was when I was born, when I was growing up, a young girl in the camp of my people. Many, oh, many times I have fled from sudden attacks upon us by the Blackfeet, the Minnetarees and other plains enemies. We Snakes lived in constant fear of them, especially in the summertime. From the going of the snow until it came again, the moons were moons of terror for us all. As I grew older, deer and elk became more and more scarce in our mountain country because of the constant hunting of them. At last, in the spring of my tenth summer, food became so scarce that we had to cross the mountains and go down to hunt buffalo or starve to death on the west side. We were then well down on a fork of *our* Big River, or as my white chiefs have named it, Snake River.

We could not wait there for the summer run of salmon. We broke camp and moved east to the west side of the pass at the head of the Missouri River. From there some of our hunters went on discovery through the pass and down the east slope and, returning a few days later, brought what meat they could pack on their riding horses. They reported that the buffalo were well below the Three Forks of the east side of the Missouri River, too far away for our men to hunt them from where we were. So our chiefs decided that we should cross the pass and go down and camp somewhere near the Forks. It was better, they said, for us to die with full bellies than to die from starvation where we were.

We crossed the pass, followed the trail running to the Great Falls and camped on the West Fork of Big River [the Jefferson], not far above its meeting point with the Middle Fork [the Gallatin]. From there our hunters went down the valley every day, always returning before sunset with buffalo meat and hides. For the first time in many moons we had enough to eat and meat to spare, which the women dried for future use — working from sunrise to sunset cutting meat into thin sheets to dry and tanning hides.

Yet all of us, men, women and children, ate and worked and played with fear in our hearts, always watching for a war party from some of the plains tribes to come into sight. We dared not sleep in our camp. As soon as the sun set and we had finished our evening meal, we scattered out, a family here, a family there, to sleep in the thick brush in the valley or up on the mountainside. My friend, that was a terrible life we led, a life of constant fear! It is the kind of life that my Snake people still live! Oh, my heart goes out to them. Just think, my friend, how I feel when I see the warriors of this village return from a raid with scalps that they have torn from the heads of my poor relatives.

One morning soon after our hunters had gone down the valley to hunt more buffalo, one of them came back as fast as his horse could carry him and shouted to us that the enemy was coming. Right on his heels came other hunters to run in our horses from the mountainside and get us mounted and started up the trail for the pass, while still others, among them my father, tried to keep the enemy back until we were well on our way. I cannot begin to tell you the confusion that our camp was so suddenly thrown into! Women and children ran aimlessly about, crying, shrieking, paying no attention to the old men begging them to take courage, to wait for the horses that were being run in and then to catch gentle ones and ride off up the trail. Some of the women ran at once for the brush with their children, and others gathered their little ones and started up the trail. Only a few of them heeded the old men and waited for the horses to be brought.

I had been playing with three or four girls, and we were a little way above camp when the trouble began. We ran down into the camp as fast as we could, and I called and called my mother, running first to our lodge, then to other places, but I could not find her. I tried to stop people and ask them if they had seen her, but they paid no attention to me, seemed not to hear me. Hardly knowing what was about, I turned and ran from camp, got into the timber and brush and made my way up the valley as fast as I could go. I soon heard the boom of guns, the shouts of the fighters off down the valley. I ran faster, if that was possible, tearing my way through the brush, often stumbling against a dead branch or log and falling flat.

Now and then I saw women and children on one side or the other of me, and I would hurry toward them, find that my mother was not with them and go on in search of her. I was a good runner. I was strong of body, but all too soon I began to tire, to run slower and slower. To my right I heard my people calling to one another, urging their horses on as they fled for the pass. I worked my way to the trail just as the last party of them were passing, and I cried out to them for help, for a horse, but they were so frightened that they never looked toward me. I stumbled on after them a little way and then turned back into the brush and went on.

At last the timber and brush on my side of the river gave out. Ahead was a long, open bottom, but on the opposite side of the river, the growth of timber continued. I looked for a place to cross the river and waded in, but the water was deep and swift. I went a long way up the open bottom before I found a shallow ford. As I started to cross it, I saw four riders coming and thought they were my people. I stopped on the shore, intending to ask them to let me ride behind one of them. Then, all too late, I saw that they were enemy riders. I ran into the river, stooping low, hoping that the bank would prevent them from seeing me as I crossed over into the brush. I did not look back; I had to watch my footing upon the slippery stones of the ford. I was no more than halfway to the brush when, above the roar of a rapid close upstream, I heard a horse splash into the water behind me, heard him make two or three jumps, heard other horses splash into the water. Then a rider suddenly seized my left arm and yanked me up on his horse in front of him. I whirled about and looked at him and tried to bite and scratch his face, but he just laughed and clasped me with his left arm so that I could not hurt him. He turned his horse about, and the three other riders turned too, and down the trail we went, they talking and laughing in their language. I was so frightened that I could not cry, no not even when we passed a boy and a girl, two of my play-mates, lying dead beside the trail!

On our way to the camp, we were joined by others of the enemy, some of them with captured horses, two of them with girl captives of my own age. Oh, how low-hearted we were, so sad and afraid of our captors, that we did not even speak to one another as we were borne down the trail.

When we arrived at camp, we found there a gathering of more than a hundred of the enemy. A few of them were holding a great band of Snake horses, others were guarding boy and girl prisoners, and the rest were going about through the camp, taking whatever they found that pleased them and setting fire to the lodges, hides, saddles, everything that would burn.

We were nine prisoners, four boys and five girls, all about my age. One of the girl prisoners named Otter Woman was my close friend. She ran to me as soon as my captor let me down from his horse, and we cried together.

She told me that she had been captured by the man who had brought me in and that he had left her with some of his companions when he went on in pursuit of our people.

While the camp was burning, our captor caught a horse for Otter Woman and one for me and saddled them with saddles that he saved from the burning. The other prisoners were also given saddled horses, and we were all soon ordered to mount and ride. We had to go. There were riders in front of us, riders behind us. We could not possibly escape from our captors by riding away from them. Down the trail we went, passing here and there one and another of our people, dead and scalped. As we passed each one, the boys and girls cried afresh, all but Otter Woman and I. We felt as badly as the others, worse, perhaps, but somehow we could not cry.

On we went down the valley and at sunset made camp beside the river. We prisoners were ordered to build a fire for ourselves and were given plenty of fat buffalo meat to roast. We did cook it but felt so sad that we could no more than taste it. All around us the war party was gathered about little fires, talking, laughing, roasting meat. There was a full moon. The night was so bright that we could see the great band of horses out on the flat, four or five men constantly riding around them and keeping them together while they grazed. We were miserable. We mourned for our relatives, dead perhaps, and we trembled as we thought of what might be in store for us — death most likely!

After a time the man who had captured Otter Woman and me came and sat near us and said in signs, "You two are mine. I shall take you to my big lodge and there you will have plenty to eat, good clothing, and you will help my women in their work. You will be the same to me as my own children. So do not be afraid of me. But do not try to escape. If you do, I shall have to kill you, for I cannot be bothered by chasing you and bringing you back.

We made no answer to that, so, looking straight at us, he went on, "How is it? Do you understand?" We signed back to him that we did.

He was a man of about fifty years and had a kind face and soft, laughing voice, but, oh, how Otter Woman and I feared him that first evening! He signed to us to lie down and go to sleep, and we did lie down around our fire, Otter Woman and I closely side by side. Then he made signs, "That is good," and moved away from us. We did not intend, any of us, to sleep. We watched the circle of our captors, hoping to escape from them when they lay down and fell asleep. But before they did that, they left three men on guard and these came and sat near us. At midnight three others took the watch and they lay down. At that, afraid though we were, we, too, slept. We were so tired we could not keep awake.

We were awakened at daylight, taken to the river to wash ourselves, brought back and given more meat and told to hurry cooking and eating it. We were now so hungry and much less frightened that we did eat. After that the horses were brought, and we were soon all mounted and on our way again down the valley. We rode steadily until noon and again, after a short rest, until night.

During the long day we had become somewhat used to our captivity and less and less afraid that our captors were going to do worse than make slaves of us. But we did not intend to be slaves. We sat around our fire that evening and made all kinds of plans to escape and return to the mountains and find our people, hiding, we were sure, somewhere in the forests of the west side. But as fast as we made our plans, we saw that they were not good. How could we escape when all through the night there was a guard over us? We could not do it! Again we became low-hearted. We cried and, crying, fell asleep.

Chapter V

The Escape of Bird Woman's Companions

On the fourth evening of our capture, we camped just above the falls of the river. That was as far as we had ever come out upon the plains with our people. On the following day we traveled until evening along a trail running across a high waterless plain and then again struck the river and made camp. Then for two days we crossed a great plain and in the evening of the second day made camp at the west end of some mountains, the Bearpaw Mountains of the Blackfeet country, as I afterward learned. Used as we were to a mountain country, the plains terrified us. We had not thought that they were of so great extent. As far as we could see to the north and the east, they ran to the edge of the world without a break. To the southeast, past a point of low mountains, they were also without end. If we did in some way escape from our captors, we saw that without horses or the means of carrying water, we should die from thirst before we could ever recross those mountains.

On that night at the point of the mountains, our captors for the first time left no guard over the camp when they lay down to sleep, and the horse herd with its guard of three or four men was out of sight behind a ridge. As soon as we were sure that we were to have no guard, we began to whisper to one another that as soon as it was safe to do so, we should one by one crawl out from camp into the dark pine forest nearby and then run for our lives.

"But where shall we run?" one of the boys asked. "We do not want to go east. We cannot go west across the waterless plain. I say that this is not the time for us to try to escape. We must wait. Anyhow, seeing that we were quiet enough this night, our captors will cease watching us and when the right time comes, we shall surely get away from them." We all agreed that the boy was right and soon went to sleep.

On the following morning, leaving the little mountain range on our right, we soon came to a small stream running in a wide, low valley in the plain. We were sure that it came from our great mountains. It was the stream that, later on, my white chiefs named Milk River. We said to one another that if we could escape from our captors now, we could follow the stream up to our mountains and then turn south along them to the Big River and then through the pass at the head of it to our people. As we rode along in the midst of our captors, we agreed to try to escape from them that night.

On that day the great number of game herds that we saw astonished us. In the wide valley and on the great plain through which it ran were grass-hidden buffalo and antelope, and in every grove of timber were herds of elk and both kinds of deer [whitetail and mule deer]. Late in the afternoon as we passed a point of timber, we came upon a big bear that was going into the timber with an antelope fawn hanging from its mouth. As soon as the bear saw us, it dropped the fawn, sat up and looked at us and then with loud roars came charging straight at us. Think of it! A bear charging more than a hundred riders driving several hundred horses! It had no fear of the thunder of the horses' feet, no fear of the odor of many men that the west wind carried. With long, swift leaps the bear came straight at us, and we all, captors and prisoners, scattered out before it and rode for our lives. Fast as we rode, it almost overtook one of us, a girl who was on a small, slow horse. The bear followed us a long way before it gave up the chase, and then when it did stop, our captors did not turn back to attack it. They rounded up the scattered herd of horses and we went on.

That evening when we made camp by the river and just below a large grove, our captors for the first time ordered us to gather wood for the cooking fires. We were afraid to go into the timber. We thought that there might be in it another of the great bears of this plains country, bears much larger than we had ever seen in our mountains. In signs, we told our captors that we were afraid. At that one of them turned upon us so fiercely that we just ran for the timber, more afraid of him than of bears. After all, we said to one another, there may not be a bear in that grove. We went into the grove a step or two at a time, farther and farther in, so far at last that we were out of sight of our captors.

"Come! Let us run! Let us go up this grove and hide in the thick willows and, when night falls, head up this valley for our mountains!" one of the boys proposed.

"We should never reach our mountains. The big bears would kill us all!" said a girl, and all the other girls agreed with her that that was true.

Said a boy, "I have been thinking hard. This is how it is with us: Were we to escape from our captors and from the bears along the way, still we should never reach our mountains, for without a bow and arrows to kill meat, we should starve to death on the long trail."

And what he said was true enough. It was true, too, as others said, that there were no roots in this country, the berries were not ripe, and we had seen only a few small fish in the river.

Then said the first boy — he was older and wiser than the rest of us, "Let us hurry and gather a lot of wood for the fires. Although our hearts are low, let us talk and laugh around our fire. So shall we make our captors think that we no longer want to escape. They will cease watching us. There will come a time when we can steal bow and arrows from them, a gun even, and then we shall do the best we can to travel back to our people."

As our leader proposed, that we did. We surprised our captors by our talk and laughter that evening. We could see them watching us, talking about us, agreeing that we were forgetting our people and the wrong that our captors had done to them and to us.

Day after day we rode on and on down that valley, once cutting a big bend in it. On the evening of the fifth day, we camped at its junction with a wide river of dirty water that we knew was the Big River we had left not far out from our mountains. Here its valley was quite wide and its groves of cottonwoods and willows of great length and breadth. Could we escape from our captors into one of the groves, we believed they would never find us.

On this evening we did not wait to be told to gather firewood. We began bringing it in from a great heap of dry drift that was lodged on a sandbar just below the mouth of the little river. There were several logs in it that could easily be rolled into the stream. We noticed that the boy who had become our leader — his name was Elk Horn — looked at them a long time and let us make a trip to camp with wood while he walked around them and upon them and, standing at one end and then another, pushed against them with the back of his legs. We were providing wood for six fires every evening. On this evening he told us to make our fire at the edge of the circle nearest the river unless we were ordered not to do so. We did make it there and were not told to move it to the center of the circle. None of our captors paid any attention to us other than to lay beside our place plenty of meat of a fat buffalo cow that they had killed while we were making camp.

After we had cooked and eaten all the meat we wanted, Elk Horn said to us, "Now I am going to tell you something. While I am telling it, little by little, do not all look at me. Look at one another, saying a few words, and do some laughing. Now I begin: If I can steal a bow and arrows or a gun after our captors fall asleep, we shall try to escape.

He stopped there, and we talked and laughed about nothing, but it was hard to do because we were so anxious to hear what more he had to say.

"At the edge of the drift pile by the river are two dry logs that we can roll into the water," he went on. "If I can get a bow and arrows or a gun without awakening anyone, we shall then, one by one, crawl away from here and down the bank of the river to the drift. When we are all there, we shall roll the logs in so that they will float. Then half of us clinging to one and half to the other, we shall push out and swim to the other shore. Of course we shall drift downstream a long way in doing that..."

There he paused while we talked and laughed again. Then he went on: "But once we get into the timber on the other side, we shall be safe. Our captors will hunt a long time for us up this side of the river and never think that we crossed it. In the shelter of the timber over there, we can go on and on up the valley, traveling in the daytime and killing what meat we need. So, if the bears do not get any of us, we shall all be again with our people by the end of another moon, maybe before that. It may not be as far to our mountains as we think. There! I have said it. Be sure all of you keep awake and watch me and one by one follow me to the drift if I leave the circle."

We all thought Elk Horn's plan a good one. One by one we told him that we should do as he said. Oh, how fast our hearts beat! Mine did, as we watched our captors, hoping that they would soon lie down and sleep soundly. Some of them did so soon after their evening meal, but others sat up smoking and talking, as long as there was wood to burn. We all lay down soon after Elk Horn had told us his plan for escape. Our fire went out, and we watched our captors, pretending that we were asleep. Would you believe it — my close friend, Otter Woman, lying by my side, almost at once went to sleep! I nudged her, pinched her, whispered to her that she must keep awake. She promised that she would and went right to sleep again! I soon knew from the way they breathed that all the others, except Elk Horn, were asleep. He was on the opposite side of the fire from me, lying on his stomach, his head to the enemy. I could see him now and then slowly raise his head and look at them. I felt sure that he would not sleep.

Two men remained up, talking and smoking long after all the others were asleep. Three or four times their fire went down to nothing but a few red coals, and they livened it with handfuls of dry twigs. As I watched these men, I found that I was getting sleepy. Two or three times I caught myself falling asleep. It was only by the greatest effort that I made myself break out of a doze and open my eyes. After the two men could find no more twigs and had lain down by their dying fire, I found it still more difficult to keep awake. Toward the last of my watch, I cast off my robe, exposing myself to the cold night air, and even bit my wrists now and then. So doing, I did keep awake and was the only one of us to see Elk Horn when he began to wriggle like a snake toward the nearest sleeping group of our captors. In the bright moonlight I could see him quite plainly. He went so slowly that he did not seem to move at all. As he neared the sleeping men, he often, as slowly, raised up and looked at them for a long time.

Watching him, I was becoming more and more excited. All feeling of sleep left me. My whole body began to tremble with eagerness for his success. When he had crawled quite near the sleepers, I sat up so that I could see plainly all that he did. Oh, how my heart went down as I saw him, after crawling close to the nearest of the sleepers, begin to back away. I thought that he was giving up, was coming back to us, that there would be no escape for us.

But no! He back-crawled only to start again, circling around to the right of the sleepers. Having done that, he crawled straight to the outer one of them. More slowly than ever, he paused by that one's side and then began backing away and, finally turning, came toward us. I almost cried out loud, "He has seized it!" when I saw that he was shuffling along with him something that he gripped with his right hand. As he neared us, I made out that it was a bow and arrow case!

It was now time for me to awaken our sleepers, but right at the start, I made a great mistake. I should have begun with my best friend, Otter Woman, lying at my side. Instead, I awakened the girl nearest me on my right, then one by one the girls beyond her. From them I passed around to the boys and one by one aroused them. I did this carefully, putting my hand upon the mouth of each one and whispering, "Awake! It is time to go!" As I awakened them, girls and boys, they one by one sat up, saw Elk Horn coming and then began crawling toward the bank of the river.

I then went back to Otter Woman, put my hand over her mouth and whispered to her to awake. She never moved. I shook her gently, whispering again and again, but all that she would do was to breathe more heavily. I dared not pinch her, nor do anything else that would make her wake suddenly and cry out. I continued to hold my hand upon her mouth and move her head this way and that and whisper, "Awake! Come, we must go!"

All that time our companions were going. I looked around and saw that they had all of them, except one other girl, the first that I had awakened, gone out of sight down the slope of the riverbank. This other girl had gone to sleep again right after I had awakened her! Oh, how angry I was at these two girls. I was minded to leave them! I did start to do so, but my love for Otter Woman drew me back to her. Again I rolled her head and whispered to her. Time and again I did that but still without effect. So finally, after a look at the sleeping men, I stood up, took hold of her two hands and began to pull her to her feet. At that she suddenly awoke, shrieking as loudly as she could, "No, no! Don't kill me!"

Ha! As one man, our captors awoke and sprang to their feet, looking around and calling to one another, and then rushing to us. Some of them seized Otter Woman and me and the other girl, Leaping Fish Woman, while others ran in all directions seeking the missing. Scared as I was, I noticed that none of them went farther than the edge of the slope of the bank. The two or three who ran to it turned and also ran for the timber above us after hurriedly looking down the slope and out at the drift pile on the sandbar. We were soon left with but one man guarding us, the man who had captured Otter Woman and me at the Three Forks of the Big River — the man who owned us. All of the others had gone off into the timber along the river and some across it into the big grove of cottonwoods running up the main river. This man was not angry at us for attempting to escape, and he did not seem to care if our companions were recaptured or went free. He just laughed at us and signed to us to go with him into the timber and gather wood, and that we should then build a fire and roast some meat.

Of course we were wondering what had become of our companions. We did not believe that they had had time to get the logs into the water and push out into the stream before our captors were aroused by Otter Woman's shrieks. We were quite sure that they had hidden in the drift pile or behind it when the shrieking and shouting began. Now as we went with the man toward the timber, I heard, surely heard, a splash in the water behind us. We all heard it, and we three looked at one another and at our captor, but he paid no attention to it.

I afterward saw that it was a sound natural to him, a dweller on this Big River. Its banks and sandbars are being continually cut and swept away by its current. It was not until I returned to my people with my white chiefs that I learned that the splash that we heard really was the splash of a log from the drift pile. Those boys and girls had hidden behind the pile and then, when all became still, got one log into the stream and, drifting far down with it, reached the other shore. From there, after almost two moons of travel, they entered our west side country and found our people. Elk Horn had no trouble killing meat with the bow and arrows he had taken from the sleeping enemy nor in making fire with a bow drill. Nor on that long trail did those boys and girls see any enemies. They did have two narrow escapes from the great bears of the Big River Valley.

We were three sad-hearted girls that sat by the fire we built for our captor. He offered us meat, but we refused it. Even the sight of it, in our despair, sickened us. As he ate his meat, our captor often broke out laughing and finally signed to us, "My friends up there in the timber are like birds running in all directions in search of their little ones. Myself, I have my little ones; here you are right with me. I wish that you could see your faces: so sad, old looking, as if you were very, very old and about to die! No, my little ones, you are not to die. You will soon be living in a good lodge, eating plenty of food, wearing good gowns. Yes, you will soon be happy enough. Come now, wipe away your tears!"

Otter Woman and I just sat and stared at him. The other girl was different. Even then, young as she was, she would get quickly, fearlessly angry. In answer to the man, she suddenly darted her head forward like a snake and spit at him. At that the man laughed harder and signed, "Now that is what I like to see, a brave heart! Women of brave heart make good wives. When you grow up, you shall surely be my wife."

In answer, Leaping Fish Woman again spat at him and signed, "I hate you!"

Chapter VI

Charbonneau Wins a Wife by Gambling

After a long time the men came straggling back from their search for our companions. A few of them caught horses, saddled them and rode away to look again for the missing ones. The rest, tired enough, lay down to sleep. Our captor made Otter Woman and me lie down close to him, and Leaping Fish Woman's captor signed her to lie beside us. We could not sleep, so great was our sorrow that we had not gotten away with our companions. When morning came and we were again on the trail down the valley, we were so tired it was all we could do to sit upon our horses.

Day after day we continued down the valley of the Big River, through great groves of cottonwoods and across wide, long, grassy bottoms that were covered with buffalo, antelope, deer and elk so tame that they would do no more than get out of the trail ahead of us. Each evening our captors killed a number of fat buffalo cows and took only the choice parts of them, leaving great quantities of meat to the wolves. We had never seen waste like that, and we expected the gods in some way to punish our captors for it. Our Snake people took every part of the animals they killed and were glad enough to eat even the toughest of the meat.

On and on we traveled and one day arrived at the village of our captors — this village in which I now stand. How we three girls did stare at it: the great, sloping, earth-roofed round lodges all enclosed with a fence of cottonwood logs set upright in the ground. How the people stared at us and we at them, at the women and girls especially, some of them wearing gowns of strange, soft, red or blue material that we were soon to learn was trade cloth. Our captors entered the village singing their war song, waving the scalps that they had taken, and were loudly greeted and praised by their people. The man who had captured Otter

Woman and me led us into his lodge, and we were surprised at the size of it and the comfort of it. There the coldest weather of winter could never be felt. What soft beds of buffalo robes there were, built all along the wall and curtained with brightly painted leather. Two women, the wives of our captor, and their children came into the lodge with us. Our captor signed to us that we were to mind them, to do all that they told us to do. One of the women, the head wife, gave us one of the couches and motioned us to sit upon it. We did so, and she soon gave us large earthen dishes full of food that she took from pots set around the fire. It was strange food, corn boiled with meat, but it tasted so good that we ate it all.

So life began for us in this village of the Minnetarees, as you call these people, the neighbors of the Mandans. That is not the right name for the Minnetarees. In their language they call themselves Hidatsa.

We got our greatest surprise that first evening when three white men came into the lodge to visit our captor. They were, we learned in time, traders from a post of the Nor'west Company somewhere north on the Assiniboine River. Two were young men, smooth-faced and blue-eyed, and their hair was sun-colored. We thought them the most handsome men we had ever seen. The other man, much older, had dark hair growing long upon his cheeks and under his nose, and that made his appearance so horrible, so sickening, that after one quick look at him, we could not look again. Somehow we were not afraid of the two young men. We liked to look at them, at their white skins tinged on their cheeks with faint red, and we could not help but admire their strangely fashioned clothes. They asked us many questions in the sign language about our people and our country. We answered them all as well as we could.

The next day our captor's women — his name was Red Arrow — set us to work tanning buffalo leather. Later we were taught to do many kinds of work. What we liked most was to work in their field of corn and other plants. It was pleasant to see the plants grow and flower and to see the flowers turn into fruit good to eat. We soon had a helper, for, as he had signed us that he would do, Red Arrow bought

Leaping Fish Woman from her captor, paying him four horses and a gun. It was his pleasure to tease her every evening, and, sad-hearted as we were, Otter Woman and I could not help but laugh with the rest at the way she would suddenly anger at him, spit at him, and say to him in sign language all the mean, taunting things of which she could think.

At first we three were always talking about escaping from these people, but as time passed Otter Woman and I became less and less eager for it, as we thought of the great dangers that we should risk upon the long trail to our country. Leaping Fish Woman was different, braver than we. She never ceased planning to escape and often told us that if we would not make the attempt with her, she would go alone. We did not believe she meant it.

The summer passed and the long winter, and by the time spring came, we had all three learned to talk in the language of our captors. As soon as the new grass began to grow, Leaping Fish Woman talked more and more about going back to our people. At last one evening, she told us that if we would not go with her, she would try to escape all by herself that very night. Fear of the long trail, the terrible bears along it and men too, Blackfeet men, was something that we could not get over, and said so, and still believed that she would not go without us.

When we awoke the next morning, she had gone! All the men of the village turned out to help Red Arrow search for her, but they found not even a footprint of her on the trails. We two missed her terribly for a long time! Then twice that summer war parties returned to the village with Snake scalps and Snake horses that they had taken in raids across the mountains. Their rejoicings over their deeds hurt us, and we were unhappy enough!

With the coming of winter, a white man who was married to a Minnetaree woman and who lived in the village below moved up to this village and bought a lodge in it. He had been a Nor'wester but was now a free man. He trapped and hunted part of the time and did some trading with the Cheyennes and other tribes that now and then came to visit the Minnetarees and the Mandans. This man — Toussaint Charbonneau — was often a visitor in our...in

Red Arrow's lodge. With other men, he came there to gamble, to play hide-the-bone for horses, guns, knives and all kinds of small property. Often, very often, we would awake in the morning and find the men still playing the game. There would sometimes be men from the lower Minnetaree village and from the Mandan villages.

The white man, Charbonneau, could not understand the language of this tribe although he had long had a Minnetaree wife, and so he conversed with the people in the sign language. When we awoke one morning, a number of men were still gambling in the lodge, among them the white man, who was playing against our captor, Red Arrow. The players were arranged in two rows, one on each side of the fire, and a man on one side of it played against the man directly opposite him. When Otter Woman and I awoke and sat up, a game had just been concluded, and the players began making bets for a fresh game. We noticed that the white man was smiling. Red Arrow appeared to be low-hearted as they arranged their bets, so we knew that Red Arrow was a heavy loser in the games of the night. The two began arguing about the bet to be made for the next game. At first Otter Woman and I, no more than half awake and sleepy-eyed, paid little attention to them. Then I saw the white man sign to our captor, "You say that you have nothing left to bet. You have several things. Plenty to bet. Your spotted buffalo runner is a good horse. My black runner is faster than he. I will bet my black against your spotted horse."

Red Arrow considered the offer for a long time. "No, I dare not bet that horse," he answered. "That horse is my meat-getter. If I should loose him, my women and children would go hungry."

"But you may win!" the white man argued. "You have been losing all night, so it is now time for you to begin winning. I really think that you will win this bet!"

Again Red Arrow thought and thought, rubbing his hands together, his forehead wrinkling deeply as he stared at the fire. I have never seen anyone frown as hard as he did. Then he suddenly straightened up and cried out as he made the signs, "No! No! I will not risk my children's food in this hide-the-bone game."

The white man laughed. "I will let you have the chance to get still more meat for your children," he signed. "I will bet my fast buffalo horse against your two Snake captives."

"Yes!" Red Arrow signed.

"No! No!" I screamed and so did Otter Woman. I had by this time learned the Minnetaree language. "Oh, Red Arrow. Oh, great chief. Good chief. Do not gamble us off! We will work for you, oh, so hard." I pleaded.

But he would not even look at us. He held the two bones, the white one and the black one. He looked down along the line of men in his row and asked them if they were ready. They were. They had all made their bets. He began juggling the bones as the gambling song was raised. He shifted them from one hand to the other in front of him, shifted them behind his back. Time and again he did this, nodding his head and bowing his back in time to the song. At last he held his two closed hands up in front of his shoulders and the singing suddenly ceased. The white man looked long at the two hands, stared long at Red Arrow, right in his eyes, stared again at the hands and then slapped his right hand into the palm of the other as he pointed to Red Arrow's left hand. As suddenly, Red Arrow sank down in his seat and, opening that hand, showed the black bone. Otter Woman and I began to cry. The white man had won us from the man who, though our captor, had been as kind to us as though we were his own children.

Red Arrow's women cried out at him, calling him names, for they had learned to love us. Red Arrow himself sat like one who had suddenly lost his mind. Then he straightened up and signed, "I will now bet my spotted fast runner. I will bet him against the two girls!"

The white man shook his head. "No," he signed. "I have won them, and I shall keep them."

"I will bet all my fourteen horses against them!" Red Arrow offered.

"No! I have won them. I shall keep them," the white man again answered. Then, turning to Otter Woman and me, he signed us to take up our belongings and go with him to his lodge. There was nothing for us to do but obey. As we followed him out of the lodge, crying harder than ever, we left Red Arrow sitting with bowed head and all humped over, his women furiously scolding him for having wagered and lost us.

Ah well! Youth quickly accustoms itself to whatever is to be. It was not long before Otter Woman and I dried our tears. The Minnetaree wife of the white man was gentle-hearted, kind to us, and we soon learned to love her. She was not strong, so we undertook to do her work. It was not long before we were doing all of it, the lodge work, the garden work, the tanning of skins, and the bringing in of wood and water. We talked less and less about trying to escape to our people. After a winter or two had passed, we never mentioned it except when a war party returned to the village with Snake scalps and Snake horses. Excepting at such times, we were contented, yes, quite happy. The white man, of winters enough to have been our father, was sometimes cross but generally good to us. His anger went as quickly as it came. So, working hard and playing not at all, we passed the winters and summers during which we grew up to be young women.

There came a time when I felt so badly that I could not talk about it. I cried and cried and was near jumping into the river to end it all! A young Mandan named White Grass, who often visited in the Minnetaree village, looked at me and I at him, for he was good to look at, slim and tall, fine of face and long-haired. From looking at one another, we came in time to saying a few words as we met and passed in the village.

One day when Otter Woman and I were tending our garden of growing corn, he came and told me that he loved me. I — I was not ashamed — I told him that I had long been hoping that he would say that to me. We sat down right there at the edge of the corn and, while Otter Woman worked, he told me what we should do. We should have a lodge of our own in the village of his people. They would build it for us and furnish it. We should have a garden of our own and raise plenty of good food, and he would hunt and bring in plenty of meat. We should be comfortable and happy. To all that he said, I answered yes, that would be the way of it. Then Otter Woman, listening to our happy talk, said to me, "Don't be crazy! Don't be making plans until you know what our white man owner will say to this."

"He will say yes, of course! I will give him ten horses for you! He cannot refuse to take ten horses, good, big horses," my young sweetheart cried.

Then I laughed happily and said that the white man would never refuse to take that many for me, more, far more, than I was worth.

But Otter Woman shook her head. "No," she said, "best that you end your dream right now, right here. He will not sell you for twenty — no, not for all the Mandan horses!"

White Grass sprang to his feet, pulled me up beside him and said to Otter Woman, "I will prove you wrong. We will go to the white man now, and I shall give him the horses!"

Away we went across the flat and into the village. We paused at the entrance to the lodge and looked at one another, for the first time afraid that all might not come out as we wanted. Then White Grass shrugged his shoulders and straightened up and led the way. Oh, how handsome he was, how fearless, as he stopped before the fireplace and said to the white man sitting on his couch, "White man! Great chief! This girl, your slave, I love, and she loves me. Ten horses, ten good, big horses I give you for her!"

The white man would not have understood what White Grass said to him had he not accompanied his talk with sign language. As it was, the white man was slow to understand, and the youth had to repeat it. Then he did understand.

He sprang to his feet and raged at the youth, who could not understand a word of his French speech. "Dog Mandan," he howled, "go away from here! Go! Go! Go! Never enter this lodge again! Outside in the village, in the gardens, the timber, wherever you see this Snake girl, go away around and never speak to her. Hurry! Get out of here!"

White Grass made no answer to that. He just stared at the still shouting, arms-waving white man and slowly turned to go. As he passed, he said to me, "Take courage, sweetheart. I go, but I shall return. I go to make a name for myself, to take horses and still more horses from the enemy, and scalps too. When I come again, he will not dare refuse to give you to me."

I, too, turned to go, go back to the corn and ask my almost-sister to comfort me. Nearly blinded with tears, I was feeling my way along when the white man thundered to me to stop and then told his Minnetaree woman to go with me to the corn to watch me and see that the young Mandan never came near. The poor, sick woman did as she was told and thereafter, wherever Otter Woman and I went, she was obliged to go with us. But her heart was not with her white man. It was with us. The next day when we were in the corn, she watched the not distant village and all who came from it, while White Grass circled in from the hills and had a last talk with me.

It was all very straight. Otter Woman sat by my side while he told me again and again how much he loved me, and I promised him that no matter how long I should have to wait, I would be his woman. He would leave the next day, he said, with a party going to war against the Pawnees and would no doubt take plenty of horses from them. That would be the beginning of his work to get together so many horses that the white man could not refuse to trade me for them. He then kissed me four times, the sacred number, and mounted his horse and rode away down the flat.

That was the last that I ever saw of my Mandan sweetheart. He had not been gone a moon before word came to us from the Mandan village that on their way to the Pawnee country, the war party which he accompanied had been ambushed by the Arickarees and all but two had been killed. The two survivors told that my sweetheart had fought bravely to the last and had killed a great warrior of the Arickarees before he fell. The white man laughed when this news came to us in our lodge, laughed long and loud and looked at me. Although I felt that my heart was going out from me, I would not let even one tear fall before him nor in any way show that this sad news was anything to me. Yes, I kept my face calm and told my almost-sister to talk with me, to say anything to keep us talking. She understood. She started the talk by asking me if I thought that the buffalo would become well furred early in the winter. But, oh, how I cried and mourned for my lost sweetheart when off in the corn or the timber, away from the white man.

Working hard, Otter Woman and I harvested the corn and other garden growths and stored them away when dry, and then we brought in load after load of firewood for winter use. Although my Mandan sweetheart was gone, the white man still had his Minnetaree woman go with us wherever we went. Day by day, moon by moon, the woman became thinner, weaker, and with the first snow of winter she took to her couch and soon died. The white man did not seem to care. He ordered us to help her relatives put up a scaffold out on the flat and lash her robe bound body upon it. When we had done that and had returned to the lodge, he said to me, "Now that the old woman is gone, you two shall be my wives. You shall be my head wife. Your place is here beside me on this couch. Your friend there shall have that couch. As you are the head wife, I look to you to keep this lodge in good shape. Yours will be the blame if there is not always garden food in the pot and plenty of wood on hand. What time you are not otherwise busy, you will tan the hides I bring in. If you are not a fool, you will make your friend work as hard as you and even harder. Now, do you understand all that I have said?"

For moons back I had seen this coming, dreading it, and now that it had come I was so scared of him that I could not answer, not even to nod my head. I was more scared than when I had been seized in the river by the Minnetaree warrior. This time I was scared to such weakness that I felt I had not the power to move even a finger. Otter Woman was scared too. She was crying. The white man went silent. I could hear him breathing hard, as he did when angry, but I could not look at him. I remained as I was, all bowed over on my couch and, oh, so sick at heart! Soon I heard him spring from his couch. He seized me and lifted me and threw me over upon his couch, crying out, "I'll teach you to mind me! Now stay there, right there where you belong!" So it was that I became the head wife of Charbonneau.

Rising Wolf paused here in the retelling of Sacagawea's own story.

"My son, Schultz," he said, "Earth Woman told me Sacagawea had got thus far in the story of her adventures when her man came in and ended it. He came in cross, cursing his luck, for he had lost the good horse we had given him.

"Yet that was nothing to what occurred the following day. About noon Sacagawea's son, a fine sturdy boy of eleven or twelve years, returned from a visit with Mandan friends in their village. His mother introduced him, and he gave me greeting in French, which he spoke with but little trace of Indian accent. Soon after he entered, his father came in and asked whose horse was tied near the lodge.

"'It is mine,' the boy said proudly. 'It is a gift from my close friend, Big Cottonwood.'

"'Ha! Is that so!' Charbonneau exclaimed, rubbing his hands and smiling happily. 'Well, my son, you shall loan him to me for a time. Last night I lost a good horse in the hide-the-button game, so I will now stake your horse against him and win him back.'

"With that, out he went, and the boy burst into tears. "'Three horses have I had,' he wailed, 'and he has gambled them off. Now he takes this one from me and will lose it. I shall never, never have a horse to keep for my own!'

"Poor lad. I felt sorry for him. My disgust at this Charbonneau grew, and my companions dispised him as much as I. Sure enough, the man did lose the horse. He came in soon after nightfall, said not a word to me, ordered his woman to set food before him and after eating, smoked in silence until bedtime. Truly that was an unhappy lodge. It depressed my companions and me. Now that he had nothing more to gamble, Charbonneau remained with us most of the time, moaning over his losses and hinting that he could recover them if we would give him something for an entering stake in the game. We did not take the hints.

"Three or four times, Sacagawea began telling me of her adventures with Lewis and Clark, but always Charbonneau took the story away from her and told what he had done and how, but for him, the expedition would never have reached the Falls of the Missouri. So I never did get her story of it all. Schultz, your almost-mother here, Earth Woman, and Crow Woman too, know it well, so let them tell it to you.

"Did Sacagawea love Charbonneau, you ask. I don't know about the love. She mothered him, was patient with him, endured his bursts of anger and was, no doubt, faithful to him to the end. For the sake of her son, whom she dearly loved, she was sure to be good to the father. She was surely good to us wanderers from the camp of the Pi-kun'-i and greatly interested in my endeavor to bring about a peace treaty between them and the Cheyennes. Yes, and it was through her own suggestion that I worked upon Heavy Robe's interest in medicines, and so I got him to become strongly in favor of a treaty of peace with the Cheyennes in order that he might see their wonderful medicines, the Sacred Arrows and the Buffalo Hat. Accompanied by the Cheyenne-Mandan chief, Big Man, we visited the Cheyenne camp on the Little Missouri and made plans with their chiefs for a peace meeting between them and the Pi-kun'-i. It took place early the following spring. It was about the grandest ceremony I ever witnessed. But all that is another story, my son. Some day you shall write the story of my life and in that will be all about our meeting the Cheyennes.

"After leaving the Minnetaree and Mandan villages for the Cheyenne camp, I never saw Sacagawea again. Years afterward at Jim Bridger's place on Green River, I did meet her son Baptiste, who had grown to be a fine upstanding man. He spoke English as well as French and was Bridger's Snake interpreter. He well remembered my visit in the lodge of his father and mother in the Minnetaree village as soon as I brought to his mind the incident of his father losing his Mandan gift horse in the hide-the-button game. He told me that his father was dead and that his mother was then living with her own Snake people. I never met Baptiste again and never heard anything more about his mother."

Chapter VII

Bird Woman Meets Lewis and Clark

Here continues the story of Bird Woman, Sacagawea, now as told by Mrs. James Kipp, otherwise known as Earth Woman:

We Mandans called Bird Woman by her Minnetaree name, Tsaka'kawia, for we well understood and spoke the language of that tribe. We also had other names for her: Gentle Woman and Led-the-First-Big-Knives Woman. My great chief father was fond of her and often got her to make long visits in our lodge and tell us about the far countries and the different peoples that she had seen in her travels. She was the only woman I ever knew who had a place in the chiefs' circle. More often than not, she sat at my father's right hand, upon his couch at the back of the lodge, at the gathering of chiefs and medicine men. We women and children, grouped near the entrance, all listened to her wonderful tales with the closest attention.

I was born the summer before the great white chiefs, Long Knife and Red Hair, arrived at our village with their men, so of course I cannot remember having seen them. Yet as I grew up I heard over and over the story of their coming, which up to that time was the greatest event that had ever happened in our villages.

When Long Knife and Red Hair arrived in our country, we had become used to white men. First, many winters before there had come to us a few white men from the north, men who wore iron shirts and carried big-mouthed guns. They came, remained with us for a time and went away promising to return, but they did not keep their promise. Many winters passed, and then came another kind of white men, the kind we later called Red Coats. North of us on the Assiniboine River, they built trading posts and asked my people to go there to trade. We could not do that. Our enemies, the Assiniboines, Crees and Sioux, barred the way. So the white men would now and then bring packtrains of goods to us and charge us terrible prices for everything that we bought.

The first white men, as my man often told me, were those of the Frenchman Sieur de la Verendrie. The next were English traders from the Nor'wester Company. Then came the greatest, the Long Knives.

Several days before they arrived, my people had word of their coming. They came, and oh, the wonder of it: their big boats with sails, the big gun in the largest boat that boomed with a noise almost as loud as thunder, the many strange utensils that the people stared at wondering for what purposes they were used. Not the least strange and interesting was the black white man they had with them, black as coal and with black, curly hair.

Soon after they arrived, our Mandan and Minnetaree and Black Moccasin chiefs held a council with the white chiefs, who gave them beautiful and valuable presents. In this council the white chiefs told why they had come to our country. They had been sent by the great chief of the Long Knives to get all tribes of Indians to make peace with one another, and they were going to make a trail westward clear to the Great Salt Water. Long Knife traders would follow this trail to bring trade goods to the different tribes living along it.

A thousand times have I heard my father and mother and Tsaka'kawia and others tell the tale of what followed that council. It is at this point that Tsaka'kawia's part in it all begins, you shall have her story of it in her own words as nearly as I can remember them. She always began the telling with a prayer to the gods.

So this is Tsaka'kawia's own story:

Pity me, gods of my people, of my far mountain country. Freshen my memory, that I may tell all I know about the great white chiefs, my good generous white chiefs, and all that happened on my journey with them to the Great Salt Water [Pacific Ocean] and back to this my Minnetaree home.

I did not attend the great council of our chiefs with the Long Knife chiefs. Women were not allowed. But my man was there, and as soon as it was over he came to me and said, "The Long Knife chiefs will winter here with us. When they go on westward, they will want a guide to show them the way and someone to take them to the Snakes in order to purchase horses from them. They will need many horses for riding and carrying their goods when they arrive at the head of the river and leave their boats."

I told him, "They cannot take their boats to the head of the river. They will not be able to get them up over the big falls, a long way this side of the mountains."

"Oh, well, wherever they abandon the boats, there they must have horses with which to go on. I shall tell them that I will be their guide and interpreter."

"But you do not know the way. You cannot even understand my Snake language," I told him.

"Fool!" he cried. "You shall show me the way, and I will lead them to your people."

Can you imagine how my heart beat when he said that? Here, after all the years, was a chance to see my own people again! At the thought of it, I cried. Otter Woman was happy too. She sprang up and danced around crying, "We are going to the mountains! We are going to the mountains! We shall see our Snake people, our dear relations."

"Come. Let us go to the Long Knives at once and tell them that we will guide and interpret for them," I said.

"No! We shall let them find out that we are the only ones who can do this for them. Then they will come to us about it, and so we shall get bigger pay than if we ran to them to offer our services," our man answered.

As our man said, so it had to be. Oh, how anxious Otter Woman and I became as the days passed and we had no word from the white men. Our man became anxious, too, and one day went down and visited the white men where they were building a fort some distance below the lower Mandan village. They said nothing to him about engaging us at that time. More long days passed. We became more uneasy, and finally our man took us down to visit the whites and to see their fort. It was not completed, but we were filled with wonder at it, the first white men's building that we had seen. They had put heavy logs one on top of another, up and up, to make the walls. As a great rock is in the middle of a river's swift current, so was that fort there in the timbered bottom. Storms could not shake it. Nor could all the warriors of our three tribes take it by attack, for there were cunningly cut holes in the walls through which the whites could shoot their many guns and kill off the attackers as they came!

The great white chiefs, Long Knife and Red Hair, greeted us and made us feel welcome in their camp. They showed their many strange things, beautiful and useful, and made us presents of some of them. They had us to eat with them too, and at that evening meal Otter Woman and I first tasted bread. We thought it the best-flavored food.

Just as soon as I looked at those two white chiefs and put my hand in theirs, my heart went out to them, for I knew that, although brave and truly fearless, they were of gentle heart. I could not keep my eyes off them. I felt that I wanted to work for them, to do all I could for them. Think then how happy I was when that evening it was arranged that we should all come and live with them as soon as their fort was completed, our man to be their Minnetaree interpreter and, at times, hunter. Nothing was then said about our going west with them in the spring, but I felt sure that would be asked of us.

A few days later the fort was completed, and we moved down with our belongings and were given a room. Oh what a pleasant place that room was, with its fireplace, windows of oiled skin and comfortable couches. The white men visited us in it, and we often visited in their rooms, especially the room of the two chiefs. They were always having visitors from the villages above and were always getting them to describe what they knew of the country and the people who inhabited it, particularly those to the west of us.

Night after night they got me to tell them about my Snake people and their country. I told them all, even to telling them how my people were persecuted by the Blackfeet, the Minnetarees and Assiniboines, and how I myself had been taken into captivity. I told them too that my people starved more than half the time, because without guns, they were driven from the plains by their powerful enemies every time that they came out after buffalo. At that Long Knife and Red Hair both told me that one of their objects in coming to the country was to make peace among all the tribes in it. If the tribes would not agree to that, the traders who would follow the trail that Long Knife and Red Hair were to make would furnish my Snake people plenty of guns. The Snakes would then be able to hold their own against all enemies.

Those were happy days for us there in the fort of the white men. I was happier than I had been, until the time came for me to have my child. Then I suffered terribly. There was another Frenchman and his family with us in the fort. I could see by the way he talked with the white chiefs that he thought I was about to die. I thought so myself, and, oh, I didn't want to die! I wanted to live! I prayed the gods to help me. At last when I thought that I could bear the pain no longer, the white chiefs and the Frenchman got together and decided to give me a powerful medicine. I took it. Soon after I drank it I gave birth to my child. Then when I found that it was a boy, I was happier than ever. And what do you think was the medicine that they gave me? It was the rattles of a poison snake crushed fine in water. It may be that I would not have drunk it had I known what it was. When all was over, I was glad that they had not told me.

From the first day of the Long Knives' arrival, the people of the Earth House tribes had been friendly. They now suddenly became less friendly, very few of them visiting the fort. I wondered why. I was soon to learn the reason. Traders from the fort of the Nor'westers on the Assiniboine River were constantly coming south to the villages with packtrains of goods and going back with furs they bought. The leader of these traders was a Frenchman named Rock, a man liked by the chiefs of the three tribes. After a trip north, he had returned with another packtrain of goods and, calling a council of all the chiefs of the Mandans, Minnetarees and Black Moccasins, he told them he had a message for them from the great chief of his company.

"These are the words of my chief," he orated. "The Long Knives who are with you are not what they would have you believe they are. They talk big, but they are nothing! Their great chief way to the east is a small chief, and theirs is a small poor people. The two chiefs now with you, Long Knife and Red Hair, make you great promises of what they will do for you. Do not believe them. They are liars. They will do nothing for you! If you wish to keep my friendship, if you wish me to continue sending trade goods to your villages, you will do nothing for them. Especially you will not furnish guides nor interpreters to help them on their way to the west. They gave you flags and medals. Throw them away and take these that I give you, for they are great medicine, while those of the Long Knives are the signs of a poor, weak, no-account people."

With that, Rock handed to the head chiefs the flags and medals and some coats of red cloth trimmed with gold braid. These last were beautiful. The chiefs thought them the finest presents they had received. In answer to what Rock demanded of them, they said they would do all that his trader chief asked. Then they went home to talk it over among themselves. Their minds were all mixed up; they did not know whom to believe nor what to do in this matter.

It was an old Minnetaree who had come to visit me that brought word of this council with Rock. At the time my man was down the river with a hunting party, but there was another Frenchman with us who was married to a Minnetaree and spoke that language. When the Frenchman came in from a hunt across the river, I got him to go with me to Long Knife and Red Hair and interpret for me. Through him, I told them all I had just learned. I could see that they were much worried about it. They said that I was a good woman to come at once to them with what I had heard and gave me some sugar and shook hands with me when I turned to go back to my room.

On the next day, Black Cougar, head chief of the Mandans, and others came to the fort. Long Knife and Red Hair said they had heard all about the council with Rock and were sorry the Mandans had believed his lies and accepted his gifts. They then explained that the Nor'westers had no right to trade south of the rivers running to the north but that, until Long Knife traders could come, which would be soon, the Nor'westers would be allowed to keep trading in the villages. Finally, they told Black Cougar and his men that there was but one great white chief, the Long Knife chief, who would be their true friend as long as they did as he asked.

In reply, Black Cougar promised for himself and all the other village chiefs that the Nor'wester presents would never be used, that in the future they would regard the great Long Knife chief as their chief and all that he asked of them they would do.

Now when my man came home and heard about this trouble, he was angry at me for having told Long Knife and Red Hair about Rock's council with the chiefs. "Men's business is not women's business," he said. "Hereafter, no matter what you learn that concerns the Nor'westers, just you keep your mouth shut about it!"

"But you are working for the Long Knives. I am your woman. It is but right that we should help them in all ways that we can," I told him.

"It may be that I shall not continue to work for them," he answered. "I do not like them. They make me work too hard. They give me too many rules to follow and not enough pay for what I do. It may be that I can fix it so that the Nor'westers will pay me a great deal just to quit the Long Knives!"

With that he went out of the room grumbling bad words, and I cried. Every day I had been expecting that the Long Knife chiefs would ask us to go west with them. Now, if they did ask us, my man would refuse to go. I had been counting upon seeing my own people again. The chances were that I should never see them. Do you wonder that I had no heart left in me that night?

More days passed. Whenever he could leave the fort and his work, my man would go to the lower Mandan village to talk with the Nor'wester traders. Finally, some of them going north after more goods took a message from him to their chief — if the chief would give him a certain sum, he would quit the service of the Long Knives. In about a moon he got his answer. The trader chief sent him word that, having quit the company when he was most needed, he could stay quit. The Nor'westers wanted nothing more to do with him. Oh, but he was mad when he got that message. But Otter Woman and I were glad. We believed that he would continue in the service of the Long Knives and that we should go west with them to our people.

More time went by, and more the Long Knife chiefs talked with us about our country, got us to make pictures of it and show them where we thought they would be likely to meet our Snake people. Then one day — oh, what a happy day that was for me — they asked my man if he would go west with them in the spring and take me along with him.

"And my other woman, Otter Woman, too?" he asked.

Long Knife pointed to her. "She begins to grow big with child," he said. "She would have it somewhere along the trail. She would be sick. No, we cannot take her. If we did, we should lose much time. We shall have no time, not a day, to spare."

"But you mistake. You do not understand," my man told him. "These Indian women are different; they are not like white women. True, my Otter Woman will have her child, but that will not delay you. She will just stop and have it, say, in the morning, and before night she will catch up."

"Even were she to do so, quickly, as you say, we could not take her," said the other chief, Red Hair. "She would take up boat room we need for our goods, and she would be one more to feed. No, Toussaint, we cannot take her."

I wanted to say something for her, but I knew that it would be useless. Had we not already learned that when these chiefs said *no*, they meant it? Otter Woman, crying bitterly, turned and went out of the room.

My man, standing by my side, was silent a long time. Then he said to the chiefs, "I can, of course, leave her with the Minnetarees, with the family of the man who captured her from the Snakes, but if I do, I shall have to pay them for caring for her. Perhaps you will pay them — a blanket maybe or tobacco, some beads, a knife or whatever?"

"Yes. We will give them something for their trouble," Red Hair agreed.

"Then it is settled. My woman here and I go with you," said my man. We went to our room, where we found Otter Woman crying.

"Cease crying!" my man shouted to her.

But she could not stop. I did all that I could to comfort her, but words were of little use. She cried all night and at times for days afterward.

At that time nothing was said as to what pay my man should get for going west with the Long Knives. Later they had some talk with him about it, but I never did know how much they promised him. At first he said that it was enough. Then he became discontented and said that it was not enough. That is, he complained to me about it but said nothing to the white men.

One day he told the chiefs that he had learned that some Minetarees camping and hunting out at the Turtle Buttes had plenty of meat to spare and that, if he were sent to them with a few trade goods, he would bring in some loads of it. They agreed to send him, and he started off with several horses, some goods and a man to help him. With a heavy heart, I watched him go. Men of the Hudson's Bay Company were trading in that Minnetaree camp, and I feared that he was just making an excuse to go to them and try to get pay from their chief to quit these Long Knife chiefs. I never learned what he said to them, but whatever it was, their answer displeased him, for upon his return, he told Long Knife and Red Hair just what was going on in the camp. The Hudson's Bay men were telling the Minnetarees that the Long Knives were a poor people and liars and thieves, and that they should kill the Long Knives. If they didn't, the Long Knives would soon steal all their land and kill off all their food and fur animals. Following that, my white chiefs told all the Indians who came to visit in the fort that they were sorry to learn that the Northwester traders were telling such terrible lies about them. Time, they said, would prove that the Long Knives were the Indians' true friends. Well, the Long Knives looked so honest when they said that and were so kind that the Indians believed them and became friendlier than they had been.

Chapter VIII

Up the Big River

Spring came and at the time the ice in the river began to break, more Nor'wester traders came to the villages with goods. This time they came with a message from their chief to my man. If he would quit the Long Knives and do all that he could to hinder their going west, he would be taken back into the employ of the Nor'wester Company.

My man considered this proposal. "The trader chief says one thing to me and then another," he complained to me, "and I don't know what to do."

"You have promised the Long Knives that we will go west with them, and you must keep that promise," I said.

"It is not a matter of promises. It is for me to determine what will be best for me," he answered and went off without telling me what he intended to do.

He soon came back and told us to pack our things as soon as we could for he had quit the Long Knives, and we were going to the upper Minnetaree village. Otter Woman and I cried as we gathered our belongings. I felt as though my head were going dead within me. I did not want to part from the kind Long Knife chiefs. Nor from my hope of taking them to my Snake people — oh, I felt that this end to my happy plans would kill me!

Late in the day we left the fort. Then, a storm coming suddenly from the north, we rode only to the lower Mandan village and took shelter in the lodge of Black Cougar.

Later Rock and other Nor'westers came. Rock said to my man, "Well, so you have really done as we wanted you to do. You have quit the Long Knives."

"Yes, I quit them," my man answered.

"How did you do it?" Rock asked.

"I put the blame of our parting upon them!" he laughed. "I said that if I went with them, it would be as interpreter and guide only, that I would not take part in the work of their soldier men, and that I should be free to take the trail back any time."

"The Long Knife chief told me, 'We cannot engage you upon any such terms as that. If you go with us, you go as interpreter, of course, and also as one of our soldiers. So you must do your share of whatever work there will be.'"

"Then we must part, and the parting may as well be now," I told them. "You can well see, I am getting on in age and am not strong enough to do hard work."

Everyone laughed, and Rock said to my man, "You old fox. You can always be trusted to get out of a tight hole."

But you can be sure that I did not laugh! That night as soon as the visitors were gone, I began to talk to my man.

"Ever since the day you won me in the hide-the-bone game," I said, "I have said to you not one cross word. I have worked hard for you. I have borne you a son. But now, though you kill me for it, I am going to tell you truth: You are a bad man, a lazy man, a liar! You made a promise to those good, kind white men and you have broken it. By doing that you have brought shame upon me and upon my son. When he becomes old enough, I shall tell him what a bad man his father is...unless you do what I ask. Now, I want you to go back to the Long Knife chiefs and tell them you are sorry, that you take back what you said, that you will go with them upon the long trail and will do as they order you to do in all things at all times."

"Shut your mouth! It's none of your business," he told me.

"I will shut my mouth now, but tomorrow I shall tell you more of your mean ways. On the next day and the next and every day thereafter, I shall tell you more and more about your mean ways, while I am making up my mind what to do — something that will make you sorry. Now sleep if you can. I don't see how it will be possible for you to sleep. Were I in your place, I should not be able to sleep. Thoughts of my badness would keep me awake!"

He did not strike me when I said that nor even answer me, so I knew that I really had set him to thinking about what he had done. I kept my promise. For three days I said something to him at every chance about his meanness in breaking with the Long Knife chiefs. Each time I promised that I was going to do something terrible because I could not bear the shame of it.

At last on the fourth day, I told him what that terrible thing was to be. "I am going to give your son and myself to the Under-Water-Gods. Watch me as you will, the chance will come, and into the deep river we will go!"

"You would not dare do that!" he said.

"If there were anything worse to do, that I would do in order to wipe out the shame you have brought upon me and upon this our son," I told him.

He made no answer nor even looked at me. He sat there in the lodge a long time thinking, thinking, and then he went out. When he came back, he did not tell me what he had done. But he had got one of Black Cougar's sons to go to the Long Knife chiefs and say to them that if they should again ask him to go with them, he would probably agree to do so. That came out when the boy returned to my man that the white chiefs had given him no answer. At that my man became uneasy. I could see his hands tremble as he filled his pipe. He looked at me and then at the fire time and again and at last said to me, "Well, have your way! You can go to your white chiefs and tell them that I am now ashamed that I left them and that I will go with them and do as they say in all things."

Oh, oh, how glad I was! I wrapped my son well and put him upon my back and ran out of the lodge. A horse was tied nearby. I never asked who owned it nor if it was gentle. I just took it and rode as hard as I could down to the fort and was let into the white chiefs' room. Their half-Indian man, Drouillard, who was a good sign user, was there. In signs I gave him my man's message. He told it to the chiefs. They laughed and shook hands with me and told me to tell my man to come back, that the trouble with him was now forgotten. They told me, too, that I was a good woman and they liked me very much. They were so kind they made me cry. I was so happy that I could not eat the food they had their black man set before me.

As soon as I could, I went out, got on the horse and hurried back to my man. I told him what the chiefs had answered. He said nothing, but went out and had the horses brought in, and back we went to the fort.

The ice now went out of the river, and everyone worked hard preparing for the start westward. The whites had built some small boats during the winter, and these were now made waterproof. Otter Woman was crying most of the time because she could not go with us. I comforted her all that I could, promising again and again to deliver to her relatives all the messages that she gave me for them. Over and over she told me that as soon as her child was born and she became able to travel, she would run away from the Minnetaree village and try to find our Snake people. I advised her not to think of doing that. I told her that if she escaped the bears and war parties that were sure to be along the way, she would die from want of food. But up to the time we parted, she insisted that she would make the attempt, for she would rather die on the trail than remain with the Minnetarees without me at her side. On the morning that our man took her to the upper village, she went almost crazy when we parted. I was so distressed that I became sick for a time.

Upon my man's return to the fort, the boats were all loaded. We had two large ones and six small ones, and we abandoned the fort and headed up the river. At the same time that we started, Long Knife and Red Hair sent their large boat down the river in charge of some of their men. It was loaded with many skins, bones and other presents for the great chief of the whites. Counting my son, we were thirty-three people in our eight boats. I was given a place in one of the two large ones.

As we went on and on up the river, sometimes making a long distance between the rising and setting of the sun, I was at times, I believe, happier than I had ever been in my life, for each day's travel brought me nearer my people, whom I so much longed to see. Then at other times, whenever I thought of what was before us, I would become unhappy. I would say to myself that we could not possibly survive the dangers we should be sure to encounter along the way. I may as well say it: My good, kind white chiefs were not cautious. They were too brave, too sure of themselves. From the start, they and their men would foolishly risk their lives by attacking all the man-killing bears that came in sight of us. At night they would build great fires that would be sure to attract to us any wandering war party that might be in the country. After we passed the mouth of the Yellowstone and entered the country of the Blackfeet, I begged my chiefs to be more cautious. I asked them to stop always a short time before dark and build little cooking fires and then after our meal, to put out the fires and then go on until dark and make camp in the darkness. But they only laughed at me and answered, "We have good guns and know how to use them. Big fires are a great comfort to us, so we must have them."

I often said to myself, "Strange are these white men. Strange their ways. They have a certain thing to do, to make a trail to the west to the Everywhere-Salt-Water. Why then are we not on horseback and traveling fast and far each day? Here we are in boats, heavily loaded with all kinds of useless things. When the wind is bad or the water swift, we make but little distance between sun and sun. We could have got all the horses that we needed from the Earth House tribes and had we done that, we should long since have arrived at the mountains. Yes, right now I should probably be talking with my own people."

And those medicine packages of theirs, packages big and little piled all around me in the boat in which I rode, how my chiefs valued them! One day a sudden hard wind struck our sail and the boat began to tip and fill with water. More and more it filled. The men in it and those on the shore went almost crazy with fear. But I was not afraid. Why should I be when I knew that I could cast off my robe and swim ashore with my son? More and more water poured into the boat and the medicine packages began to float out of it. I seized them one by one as they were going by and held them, and when at last we reached the shore, my good white chiefs acted as though I had done a wonderful thing in saving their packages. It seemed as though they could not thank me enough for what I had done. Thinking about it after it was over and when the things had been spread out to dry, I said to myself, "Although I cannot understand them, these little instruments of shining steel and these writings on thin white paper must be powerful medicine. Hereafter, whenever we run into danger, I shall, after my son, have my first thought for their safety and so please my kind white chiefs."

After leaving the mouth of Little River or, as my white chiefs named it, Milk River, we went up through a part of the Big River Valley that I had not seen, for when I was captured by the Minnetarees, we had, after leaving the valley at the mouth of Bear River, struck across to Little River and followed it down. We were many days in getting the boats up this long, winding and ever swifter part of the river. The farther up we went the more I looked for signs of the Blackfeet and their war brothers, the Big Bellies, but look as I would, I could not find a single footprint they had made nor any tracks of their horses. I thought that strange. When we arrived at the mouth of the stream, my white chiefs named it the Musselshell. Some of the men went up it in the afternoon and, returning, told of a stream coming in from the plain on the right. My chiefs then told me that it should have my name, as they called it Sah-ka-ga'-we'ah.

I asked my man to tell them that I wished they would give it my right name, Bo-i'-naiv, Grass Woman.

But he laughed at me and answered "Never mind! It does not matter what they call it!"

I thought it did matter, but I was bashful about asking them to make the change.

"It seemed to matter when they named a creek after you," I said to him. "You were pleased enough!"

"Yes, but I am a man! Important! Women...their names to things do not matter," he answered. I said nothing more.

It was some days after passing the mouth of the Other-Side-Bear-River, the Musselshell, that we arrived at the mouth of a small river coming from the south and there came upon a not long deserted campground of the enemy — either Blackfeet or their war brothers, the Big Bellies. There had been a great camp of them at the mouth of the small river and another opposite it on the north side of Big River. Just below the smaller, they had decoyed a herd of buffalo over a cliff to death, and wolves were still eating the meat of old and poor animals the hunters had not thought worth taking. As I looked at the abandoned fireplaces of the camp, I said to myself, "It will not be long before we are discovered by the enemies who were recently here. When that happens our end will come! Brave though my white chiefs and their men are, they are too few to win a fight with the hundreds of warriors who will come against them!"

My heart was low as we went on up the river. I felt that, after all, I was not to see my country and people again. I made up my mind that I would not be captured again. Before the enemy could lay hands upon me, I would kill my son and then myself. I now kept constant watch of the river bottoms ahead and the tops of the cliffs on each side of the valley, expecting at every turn to see the enemy approaching.

At last one morning we came to the mouth of Bear River [Marias River] and made camp. I was now in country that I knew! Here I had left Big River with my Minnetaree captors and struck off across the plain to Little River. On horseback it was but a day from here to the falls of Big River. Look as I would, I could find no fresh signs of the enemy, not a fireplace, not a track of man or horse, and I began to think that we might after all reach the mountains without being discovered by the Blackfeet. I prayed for that! Oh, how I prayed the gods to keep the eyes of the enemy from us while we went on and on to the head of the river and over the mountains to my people!

To my surprise, after my white chiefs had made medicine with their strange instruments, we did not go on. One of the chiefs went up Big River and the other up Bear River, each with a few men, leaving us to be easily killed by the enemy should they discover us. Red Hair, who went up Big River, was gone from us three days. Long Knife, who went up Bear River, did not return until the evening of the fifth day. After his return, we remained there still another day, drying our things after the heavy rain that had fallen, hiding some of them in a hole the men dug in the ground, and leaving one of our boats on an island. And why do you think they were gone so long up the two rivers? They were all that time learning which of them was Big River, the one that they wanted to follow! And there I was. I could have told them which one it was, but they had not asked me! When my man told me what they had been doing, I scolded him and asked him to tell Long Knife and Red Hair that I was sorry they had not told me what was their trouble, for I could have saved them these five days of wandering. He would not do it.

"I can't. They would then blame me for not having asked you about it," he answered. That is one great fault in men — they think that women are so foolish that it is a waste of time to question them about anything!

On our last night at the mouth of Bear River, I fell sick. While I slept, some Blackfeet or other enemy ghost wandering there had found me and put its badness into my body. As we went on up the river, I became sicker day by day and began to think I was about to die. If I did, then my son, lacking the milk of my breast, would die too. I said to myself that for his sake, I must not die. I prayed the gods for help. I made a sacrifice to them. I begged them to sustain life in me until I could reach their stinking-water spring at the falls and drink its healing water. They did help me as I fought the ghost's evil inside me. At last when we neared the place, I told my man where the spring was and sent him to bring me water. I drank and drank, and by the time we went into camp near the spring, I began to feel better. Two days later I was worse again, but I continued to pray to the gods and drink the medicine water. Finally the evil work of the enemy ghost went from me.

I had thought that when we arrived at the long stretch of falls and swift water in the river, we should abandon the boats and go on to my country on foot. But no! As soon as we arrived at the first of the bad water, the men began at once to cut down a big tree from which to saw round pieces upon which to draw the boats — all but the largest one — the long, rough and steep way to the almost-still water above the upper falls. This caused a long delay, many days of hard toil. While their men worked dragging the boats upon the log slices up the trail and carrying the many packages of goods upon their backs, Long Knife and Red Hair made medicine with their queer instruments at each of the falls, not once but many times. I could not understand why they did that. It seemed to me useless work. They were making a trail to the west. Well, no boats nor men could go up over the falls, so why not plainly mark the beginning of the trail around the falls and its end up at the still water and be done with it? That was the one fault with my good white chiefs — they were time wasters.

At last a camp was made above the falls, and one day we in the lower camp started out to move the last of the boats and the goods packages up to it. I went ahead of the party with Red Hair, the black white man and my man. It was a bad day, low black clouds everywhere shutting out the blue and rain falling. We had not gone far on the trail when there came a terrible wind and hardest rain. The black white man was ahead. Red Hair, my man and I ran down into a coulee and stood under a rock wall that formed its right bank. The rain came harder and harder until it made the day so dark that we could no more than see the other bank of the coulee not ten steps across from us. I knew that so heavy a rain would soon make a river where we stood and was about to tell my man that we had best get out of the coulee, when suddenly we saw a great flood coming down upon us. I had set my son down at my feet, spreading his wraps upon his carrying case for him to lie upon, and as I snatched him up, Red Hair and my man seized hold of me and we made a run for the steep bank across the way. Before we could reach it the water began to rise and foam about us and roll stones that bruised our legs and nearly took us off our feet.

Who do you think it was that saved me and my son? My man? No. By his hard pulling and pushing, Red Hair saved the three of us from being taken by the rise of roaring water and stones down the coulee into Big River and down it to our death in the falls! Can you wonder that I loved Red Hair more than ever? When I was sick he tried to doctor me. He was always doing something for me and my son. Now he had risked his life to save us from death in the flood. He was a real father to me. From that time on to the end of our long trail, I did all that I could for him.

My man, Charbonneau — I have said some hard things about him. I shall say some more, but do not think that I hated him. He was the father of my child. He was a child himself — for all his bigness and strength, nothing but a child. So I pitied him and did all that I could for his comfort, although at times it was hard.

I had thought that when we got the boats and the goods packages to the head of the falls, we should at once go on. But no! The men were putting a covering of skins upon a boat frame of iron pieces which had been brought along for that purpose, and when they finished it, found they had wasted their time. Water leaked into it faster than they could bail it out! So then, more small boats had to be built, and that took more time. I began to think that winter would set in before we could reach the mountains. Up the river two cottonwood trees were found from which boats could be made, and Red Hair took some of the men there and set them to work. The rest of us were several days moving to the place, and a part of the way I went on foot with Long Knife and another.

Before we got to camp, fear struck me again, for we came upon a recently deserted camp of the enemy, either Blackfeet or Big Bellies. In the center of it they had put up a great lodge to their gods, the poles of which were cottonwood trees so large and heavy that I could not understand how they had managed to raise them. That night in my sleep, I saw the enemy warriors making sacrifices to their gods there in the lodge, and I saw them dancing and waving fresh Snake scalps that they had taken. When day came and I sat and looked at the mountains, as I had been doing for some days, I said to myself, "No, my people, you are nowhere there on those slopes! The enemy camped here. They have hunted you out, killed some of you and driven the survivors back across the range, there again to starve!" I was sad-feeling for days afterward. I no longer watched the valley and its slopes for the possible appearance of my people, sneaking out from the mountains to kill a few buffalo. I watched instead for the enemy, expected them to appear at any time and charge into our camp and kill all of us.

At last the two new boats were finished, and we loaded the old and the new ones and again set out westward. We were now in country I well knew — every bottom, bend and slope. Memories of what had here happened and there, in my girlhood days, made me laugh at times and at times cry. That is I did so at first. Then I took strong hold of myself. "If you act this way," I said, "Red Hair and Long Knife will think you have gone crazy." Thereafter, no matter how I felt, I gripped the boat hard and hard shut my teeth and so made myself appear as calm as a lakelet on a windless day.

As we made our way up into the mountains, the river became swifter and our progress slower. More than ever I hated the boats. At times it was hard for me to keep from leaving them, from taking my little son upon my back and hurrying on in search of my people. At every camp we made I looked for signs of them. Then one day we came to a place where they had been camped. Oh, how glad I was when I saw that camp, for I had feared that they were all dead, had all been killed by the people of the plains. But no! As usual, they had been out after buffalo during the winter and with the coming of summer had made their way back into the mountains. I could tell by the growth of grass around the fireplaces that they had camped here in early spring. I wondered how far back they had gone. I feared that they had gone through the pass and then away to the south. If they had, we should never see them.

One evening soon after we had come upon a second old camp of my people, Red Hair and Long Knife held a long council with some of the men. My man was in it, but he did not tell me what the talk was about. I did not learn until the next day after Red Hair and his black white man and two others had left us, that it had been decided they should go ahead to try to find my people and make friends with them. I was angry when my man told me that. "Why am I here but to do that very thing!" I scolded. "Should my people see Red Hair and his men approaching, they would run and hide, perhaps lie in wait and kill them. But if I were with them, it would be different. I would travel far in the lead and make myself known to my people as soon as I sighted them, and then all would be well with us."

It was the following day or the day after that we saw a great smoke rising from a mountain slope far ahead of us. As it rose into the blue, my heart almost went dead within me. "There! Now you have done it!" I scolded my man. "By not telling me what you were counseling about with our chiefs, it is you who will be to blame for whatever happens! That big smoke is a sign smoke of my people. It warns all who see it that enemies have been discovered and that all should retreat at once back into the mountains. It is your fault! Had I gone with Red Hair, this would not have happened!"

"Woman, just you mind your woman business and I will mind my man business!" he answered.

I could say nothing more. I felt too sad, too sick to talk.

Red Hair and his men were gone from us three days, during which we kept boating up the river. When we met them, they told us that they had gone as far as the grass burning, but had seen no Indians nor any fresh signs of them. I said nothing to that. I knew very well that my people had seen them and had retreated from them without leaving a trail that could be followed. Some days later after another council, Red Hair again went on ahead with a few of the men, and this time my man went with him. I knew nothing about the council until the following morning when my man took up a blanket and his gun and started off, saying to me, "I go with Red Hair in search of your people. If they are in the country, I shall find them." Yes, that was all that he said to me. Ever since I had scolded him, he had been angry at me. He was jealous of me; he wanted to be the one to bring about the meeting of the Long Knives and my Snake people. I almost could have laughed. He was such a child in many of his ways.

This time Red Hair and his followers were gone six days without having found my people nor fresh signs of them. Both Red Hair and my man had become sick, and in crossing a stream my man had come very near drowning. Also he had got sore feet. Again I almost laughed when he came limping to where I was by the fire and sat down with much groaning and in a small voice asked me to give him food.

We had this day passed the meeting place of the three rivers that make Big River and were camped right where, many summers back, my people were camped when the Minnetarees attacked us. When our evening meal was over,

I took my son upon my back and went all over that camp-ground. I found the stone ringed fireplace that my mother and my sisters and I had made, the one in which we had built our last fire together and cooked our last meal for our men and for ourselves. I sat down before it and touched those stones that my mother and sisters had placed there and cried. Where were they, my relatives? Was it possible that they were still alive? Oh, how I prayed that they were and that I might soon meet them somewhere up there in the great mountains.

We remained in this camp several days and then, after resuming our way, soon came to the place where the Minnetaree had pursued me into the river and snatched me up before him on his horse. A hundred times I had dreamed about it, awaking with shrieks of terror! A hundred times I had seen the place with my dream eyes and now saw it with my awake eyes and could see no change in it since that terrible day of my capture. No, there had been no change in it. The crumbling bank sloping down to the ford was still there. The wide swift water on the ford was no deeper. The timber on the far shore remained as it had been, untouched by fire, unswept by the floods of spring. But I had changed. I was no longer the girl who had been snatched up out there in the river and had tried to scratch and bite her captor as she was borne away. Right there I asked myself if I was sorry that I had been captured, and I had to answer that I was not sorry. True, I had suffered much at first, but my captor — all the Minnetarees — had been good to me. True, I had lost my Mandan sweetheart, and I had not wanted to become the white man's woman, but those sorrows were over. During all the winters and summers since I had been carried away from this place, I had lived in warm lodges, safe from all enemies, had been given plenty of food and clothing, and best of all, I had become a mother. I had my son snuggling warm at my breast. What I had suffered from being taken from my people was nothing to the happiness I had gained through having him. Had I not been captured, I should never have met these great white chiefs with whom I was traveling and for whom I felt that I would die if that were necessary for their happiness. They were so great, wise, brave and good that at times I felt that they must be more than just men.

After passing the place of my capture, Long Knife took my man and several others with him and set out ahead to try to find my people. I asked Long Knife to allow me to go, too, but that was not to be. He answered that he would gladly take me along with my man were it not for my son. With him to carry and care for, he believed that I could not stand the hardships that they were sure to encounter. So they went and were absent from us a number of days, coming to our camp again as we were passing the Beaver's Head. They had found no fresh signs of my people. My man was worn out, his feet very sore. I gave him some marrow grease to rub into them.

The following day Long Knife again went ahead with three men, taking the half Indian Drouillard in place of my man, for he, too, was a good sign talker. Again I begged to be taken with the lead party, for we were now right up to the edge of the country of my people, and I feared that without me to explain that they were friends, my people would attack and kill them. I had known ever since I had seen that smoke signal some days back that my people were aware that we were moving up the valley and that, of course, they believed we were an enemy war party. As I entreated Long Knife to take me with him and his men, I could see that he had a mind to. I felt hopeful he would. Then my man told him that he did not want me to go, that with my child my place was in the boat. That ended it. Long Knife laughed, said something to Red Hair, told me that he was sorry he could not take me along, and then departed with his men. I was so disappointed that I cried!

Chapter IX

With Her Own People Again

Days passed. We made slow progress up the swift and now often shallow river, so shallow that for most of the time, I walked ahead on the shore while the men dragged the boats over the bars. One morning, as soon as the start for the day was made, Red Hair and my man and I went on ahead of the boats. We had not traveled far along the shore when I discovered some riders hurrying toward us. I could see their faces. I did not recognize them. How could I after all these winters? But by their dress, by the shape of their bodies, I knew that these riders were my own people, some of them perhaps my own relatives.

I raised my hand to them in greeting. I cried out to them, "My people! My people! I am your long lost Grass Woman!"

Then I whirled around and signed to Red Hair, who was behind me, "These are my people. These are my people." Then I turned again and ran to meet them, crying, laughing and so happy, so filled with happiness that I went almost crazy with it.

Now I saw that our half-Indian man was with them, that he had on Snake clothing, and by that I knew that Long Knife was safe, that my people had not killed him. I felt that the gods had been more than good to us, that more happiness than I had right then would kill me.

Now we met, these riders and I, and again I called out my name. They cried, "Yes! Yes! We know you, Grass Woman. This is a great day! This is a medicine day, this day of your return to us!" Then they raised our Snake song of greeting and happiness and turned and went up the bottom with us, around the bend toward their camp where, one of them told me, a number of my people, with the white chief and his men, awaited our coming.

As we neared the place, some women advanced to meet us and when they had come near, the lead one stopped suddenly and stared at me, and I stared at her. Then crying, laughing, crying, we ran together and hugged and kissed one another. "It is you! It is you, Grass Woman!" she cried.

I could not answer. I could not speak for the happiness, for this was Leaping Fish Woman, she who had so long since fled from the Minnetaree village. I had often thought of her, mourned for her. I had not believed that she could possibly escape the dangers of the long trail that she had to follow. Yet here she was! But, oh, how thin she was. Hunger stared at me out of her big, sunken eyes. I could see it in the eyes of the other women who came running to embrace me. It was with my people as it had ever been. Yet out on the plain were countless herds of buffalo! How I wanted to help them, my persecuted, defenseless people!

We could not let go of each other, Leaping Fish Woman and I. We stood in close embrace, she asking me questions, the other women standing close around listening. Then suddenly my man came and hurried me to where the Snake warriors were gathered with Red Hair and Long Knife in a small, poor lodge of willow brush. I was wanted to interpret for them. As I took my seat near the entrance and laid my son down in his wrappings, the chief asked one of his warriors to pass him a small pipe loading stick. His voice sounded much like one that I had known but somewhat deeper. I looked up at him. I knew him. He was my elder brother!

I sprang across to him, crying "Oh brother! Oh Black Bow! Elder brother, don't you know me? I am your sister, Grass Woman." I put my blanket around his shoulders and embraced and kissed him. I could feel him tremble.

"So you are!" he answered. "I recognize you. I am glad! But take courage. There must be no tears on my face before these white chiefs. Take courage, sister, and interpret for us."

"I will try to do so," I answered. "But just think, brother! After all these winters I am here with you, here where I thought I was never again to come."

"Yes, truly the gods have been kind," he answered. "But now dry your tears. Interpret to me the words of these white chiefs. After the council is ended, you and I will talk."

At that I tried my best to stop crying. Long Knife said a few words to my man, who interpreted them to me. Then I began to tell my brother what had been said. My thoughts were too much for me. I could not stop crying. I could not even remember what I was to interpret. My man got angry at me; called me bad names. But Red Hair and Long Knife took pity upon me. They saw how I felt and halted the council, saying that they would put it off until I was myself again. They arose and went out. I was left with my brother.

"Tell me all. Tell me about our family," I said to him.

"Our father was killed on the day that the enemy took you from us," he said.

"Yes, I know. I saw him dead and scalped beside the trail," I told him.

"Our mother is dead and our two sisters. Our sister Red Willow Woman left a little boy. Our brother is not here. I sent him to one of our tribes with a message."

"Where is the little boy?" I asked after I had cried more.

"In our camp on the other side of the pass."

"Brother, give him to me. Let me be his mother. I will be a good mother to him," I said.

"Take him. I know that you will be good to him," he answered. Thoughts of what I should do for the little one helped me dry my tears.

My brother began asking me many questions. He wanted to know about the Minnetarees, how many they were, how many guns they had and where they had obtained them. After I had answered these questions and told him much that he had not asked, he said to me, "Truly the gods are good to us. Here you are returned to your own people. Here are these white men with many guns and much food for us. No longer shall we starve. I have sent messengers to all the tribes of our people and to the Flatheads, asking them to come and help us kill these white men. When we have done that and have taken their guns, we shall go out upon the plains and live there, for we shall then be able to kill off the plains enemies when they attack us."

When my brother said that, I thought he was joking. I looked at him, saw that he meant what he had said. My body went cold. What? Kill my good chiefs and their men?

Here was a terrible situation! And it was my own brother who was planning to do this! What could I say to him to make him change his mind? I prayed the gods to help me and began... "Brother, these two white chiefs and their men have been good to me. If you kill them, I too must die."

"What are their lives compared to the lives of our people?" he cried. "Nothing! Only by killing these white men and taking their guns can we go out and hold our own against our enemies on the buffalo plains!"

"For how long?" I asked. "After just one fight with your enemies you would have used all the food for the guns. Then what would you do? Could you make more of the black sand and the heavy round balls? No, you could not! After you had killed many of the enemy, those who survived would go home and gather together all the warriors of the three tribes of the Earth House people. The number of those who would come to attack you would be as many as the grass. Not one of you would live to see these mountains again!"

"But you can help us. You must!" he cried. "You have been with the white men a long time and have seen them make gun food. You shall teach us how to make it."

"Not even Red Hair and Long Knife, great chiefs though they are, know how to make the black sand," I told him. "I have inquired about that and have learned that the making of it is a secret known only to some white medicine men who live far in the east."

My brother groaned and humped over in his seat.

I saw that I had hit him and went on. "I know these white men. Their talk is as straight as the straightest pine tree that you ever saw. They do not know how to lie. They say they have come to make a trail from the far east to the shore of the Everywhere-Salt-Water, to make peace with the different tribes along the way and to get the tribes to make peace with one another. They promise that white traders shall follow this trail and bring you plenty of guns and gun food and plenty of all the useful and beautiful things of white men's make. Brother, be wise! Do that which is best for us all. Send messengers at once to tell the warriors of the different tribes to remain where they are, for the white men are not to be attacked."

"You will not tell your white chiefs about this?" he asked.

"I should be ashamed to let them know that my brother had so foolishly made plans against them," I answered.

"I was foolish," he agreed, "but I meant well for my people. I just thought of the many guns we should get. Why...oh why didn't I see at once that they would become as useless to us as the few that we have as soon as the black sand that we should take with them should be used up! Yes. I will send a man at once to our camp on the other side of the pass. He shall send messengers from there to the tribes to tell them we are not to fight the white men."

At that he called a young man to us, and we both explained to him what he was to do. Away he went to camp to send out the messengers. So were my white chiefs and their men saved from sudden end there in the mountains.

That afternoon Red Hair and Long Knife held a great council with my brother and his men. They told why they had come to the country, what they would do for them, especially promising that traders should soon come to them with all the guns and things that they could use. They gave my brother and his head warriors beautiful presents and to all several small presents. Then they asked that horses be furnished them upon which to pack their goods and so enable them to go on their way to the Everywhere-Salt-Water, agreeing to pay well for all the horses that they bought. My brother answered that he and his men would furnish the horses needed, and the council came to an end.

There were here, at the end of our boat trail, only a few of my people. They had not with them enough horses with which to pack all our goods to the camp on the other side of the pass. On the following day, therefore, Red Hair and some of the men started out for the camp with my brother and his people, taking what horses had been bought. Long Knife and the rest of the men remained at the river to wait until they could be provided with horses. My man and I went with Red Hair and my brother's party. I rode. Red Hair, kind, generous man that he ever was, had given my man goods with which to buy a horse for me!

We were nearly three days in making the camp, which was on the west slope of the great mountains. But those days were not long to me. I knew every part of the trail. Every place along it that we passed brought to me remembrance of some happening there in my young days. At last we arrived at the camp, and people old and young came crowding around me to tell me how glad they were to see me after the many winters that had passed since I had been taken from them.

Among them came an old man crying loudly, "Make way for me! Make way! Where is that woman, Grass Woman? Show her to me. She is mine. Her father gave her to me long before she was carried off by the enemy war party!"

"Here I am," I told him, "but I am not your woman! See, there he is, my man, and this one on my back is our son."

The old man was nearly blind. He felt his way toward me with his staff, put his hands upon me and tried to see my face, and then felt of the roundness of the child. "It is true! She has a child!" he said. "Well what if you have? You still belong to me! But I do not want you now. Give me tobacco and I will let you go. Yes, give me tobacco and you can do as you please with yourself."

I told my man what he had said. The old man got a piece of tobacco and went stumbling away with it, saying over and over to himself, "Women! Of what use are women to me? Tobacco! Ha! Tobacco is what makes happiness!"

I now had no idle time. When I was not interpreting for Red Hair, I was talking with my people, telling them about the Earth House tribes, how they lived, how well fed they were, and how comfortable their lodges. Most of all, my people were interested in what I told them about the game we had seen at the falls of the Big-River-of-the-Plains. My brother became greatly excited, "There they are, thousands and thousands of buffalo only a few day's journey away and here we are starving. Even though we die for it, we must go out there and kill buffalo!" he said. All agreed with him that this was the one thing for them to do and do at once.

How sorry I felt for them, my own people, starving. There wasn't enough meat in all that camp to make a meal for a dog. To me, after my fat living in the Minnetaree village and upon the long trail from it, the few handfuls of roots that they found each day were mean and pitiful.

I now got my brother and others to tell Red Hair all that they knew about the country to the west and the trails in it. None of them had been very far to the west and so could tell him only what they had heard, and that was very little. It was Red Hair's plan to go down the stream [Salmon River] from where we were camped to where it joined the river which, far off, ran into the truly Big River Columbia River], and there to build boats in which to make our way to the Everywhere-Salt-Water. An old man told him that he had been down that stream for some distance and that, as far as he had gone, it had been too rough for boats. My brother and others told him that the one way to get to the Big River, where boats could be used, would be to go north to the Nez Perces' trail to the buffalo plains and follow it west to Big River. When they struck it in the Nez Perces' country, they could then build boats or buy them from boat tribes just west of the Nez Perces and travel in them down the Big River to the Great Water.

Red Hair considered what he had been told and answered that he must see for himself if the near stream was too rough for boats. So, engaging the old man to show him the way, he set out down the creek with his men the following day. On the next day following that, my brother, my man and I and many of the people set out to take horses to Long Knife and bring him and his men and goods across the mountains to this camp of my people. When we arrived at Long Knife's camp, he bought all the horses that my people could spare, but they were not enough with which to make the start. So we waited for another party of my people to come with more horses. They arrived on the next day and sold all the animals that they could let go. Still we had not enough. So when we did make the start west, after sinking our stone-loaded boats deep in the water, what goods the horses could not carry were carried by some of the women. We got a late start and made an early camp.

On the following day after breaking camp, I rode up beside my brother and asked him why early that morning he had sent two young men on ahead of us.

"I have sent them on to tell the people to break camp and come east," he answered. "We are all starving. As soon as we meet, we shall all band together and strike out for the buffalo plains. We have now some black sand and some balls for our guns, given us by one and another of your chiefs' men. So even if we do meet a war party of the enemy, we shall manage to kill a few buffalo and bring the meat back here to the mountains."

Now when my brother told me that, I just went sick with shame for him! He has promised Red Hair and Long Knife to furnish all the horses needed to take them and their goods to the west side camp where they would buy all the horses they wanted, horses they must have to enable them to go on westward. Here he was planning to gather his people and turn back with them to go down to hunt buffalo! I was so angry at him that I could not speak. Then it came to me that I was not the one to reproach him. Only too well I knew that men seldom pay attention to women's advice. The one thing for me to do was to tell Long Knife what was happening and let him scold my brother.

"Yes, with the black sand and balls that we now have for our guns, we can risk going out after buffalo," my brother went on, a happy smile on the face that he turned to me. "Myself, I have all of thirty swallows of black sand and balls. Your man is generous. He gave them to me."

At that I became angrier. My chiefs had warned the men not to give nor sell a single load of powder and ball to the Indians, and my own man was one of those who had disobeyed the order! I said to myself that right here our trail making would end, for without the horses that we needed, we could not make our way onward toward the Everywhere-Salt-Water. Almost then I let loose at my brother the anger within me. Then I said to myself, "No. I cannot scold him! What had his people to eat this morning? Most of them a few roots. Some of them not a mouthful of anything. Were I in his place, I should think as he does, that food for his starving people is of more importance than the wants of a few white men. But this must be: As the people have starved, so must they starve a few days longer. My white chiefs have got to have the horses that they need!"

I dropped back beside my man leading one of the pack horses and told him what my brother had done. I did not tell him I knew that he and others had given powder and balls to my people. What was done was done. I should never tell my chiefs. We already had enough troubles!

My man did nothing but say bad words when I had told him what was happening. He called my brother all the bad names he could think of. Then he turned upon me, "And so you think that if your brother carries out his intention, we shall turn back! You should know better by this time these two white chiefs you love so much. Nothing will stop them! If they can't get horses they will still go on, forcing us along with them. I shall have to go afoot, on and on until somewhere there in the west I fall and die!"

"And by your fault and serve you right! You would give away your powder and balls!" I almost told him but stopped my tongue just in time and said instead, "I still have faith in my white chiefs to do all things. You must hurry on and tell Long Knife what my brother has done."

It was not until a midday rest that we caught up with Long Knife. As soon as my man told him what my brother had done, Long Knife called a council and, of course, I had to do the interpreting. Do you think that it was pleasant for me, turning into the language of my people his scolding of my brother? Long Knife told him that he was a man of two tongues and terribly shamed himself before all the people. I could not tell my brother all that he said. I had not the heart. In the worst parts, I put in some half pleasant words of my own and made my brother tell Long Knife that he was sorry for what he had done, that so anxious was he to get his people started out for food he had not remembered his promise, and that he would at once send a messenger to tell the people at the west side camps to remain where they were until we arrived. And so that trouble was wiped out.

When we arrived at the camp of my people at the west end of the pass, we learned that another camp of them, gathered from different fishing places, was not far below, and that Red Hair and his men were there. They soon joined us, and we learned that Red Hair had been down the stream a long way and had found it too rough for boats.

An old man named Diving Eagle had been Red Hair's guide. He was a member of a tribe of our nation that lived far to the west and had traveled to many places and visited many tribes. He now said that we must go north to the Nez Perces' trail to the buffalo plains and follow it west until we arrived at a place where we could build boats in which to travel the rest of the way to the Everywhere-Salt-Water. Red Hair and Long Knife decided that we should do this, and we prepared to go. All the horses were bought that my people could spare, but still we had not all that we wanted. The Blackfeet and the Minnetarees had stolen most of my people's horses. The last two that we got were bought at a high price, a gun, a pistol and much food, and even at that, the owners did not like to let them go.

Although he said nothing to me about it, my brother counted on my man's and my parting from Red Hair and Long Knife and turning back with him to the buffalo plains.

I was surprised when he now said to me, "Tomorrow your white men go. I have by my waiting on them delayed taking my hungry people out to meat. You had better get your things out from the white men's camp this evening so that we can make an early start in the morning."

"What do you mean?" I asked. "I have had no thought of turning back with you. What made you think that I should?"

I talked with your man about it. He doesn't understand signs well, but I understood him to say that you and he would leave the white men and join us," he answered.

My man was right there with us, and I asked him what he had said to my brother.

"I told him that I didn't want to go any farther west," he replied. "Nor do I. I have gone far enough with these white men. I have slaved enough for them. It is best that we leave them right here!"

"We cannot do it. You promised them that we should go with them to the Everywhere-Salt-Water and back to the Minnetaree village. You put your name to that promise, and what was written cannot be rubbed out!" I said.

"There is a way out of it," he told me. "You can become sick, very sick, too sick to go on with them. Then, of course, I shall have to leave the party and take care of you."

"I shall not be sick! I am strong to go on!" I said.

"Well, if you don't care for yourself and for me, you ought

to care for our son," he pleaded. "We are almost starving now and from all that I can learn, to the west there is no food at all after the fish turn about and go down the rivers. If we go on, we go to die from starvation!"

"Then we die with Red Hair and Long Knife, with good company!" I answered. "But we shall not. To the west are many tribes of people, and where they find food, we can."

"Some of those tribes are powerful. If we escape starvation, we shall be killed for the goods that we take with us,"

"You know as well as I do," I answered my man, "that Red Hair and Long Knife are great chiefs, that they have powerful medicine, that their men are brave. Enemy tribes cannot stop them from doing what they have set out to do!"

At that my man sprang up and without another word to me went off to the other camp.

I then explained to my brother why we could not leave the white men and asked him to take care of my adopted son until I could return to care for him myself. He promised to do that and said that he had taken the best care of him since his mother's death.

And so we parted. I felt very sad as I walked back to our camp. I thought of the terrible risk my people were about to take in going out after buffalo. Although I had talked bravely enough about it, I too feared the long trail that we were about to follow into the west.

Chapter X

To the Everywhere-Salt-Water

We broke camp early the next morning, my people striking out to the east, we to the west and north. Old Diving Eagle, his sons and a young man going with a message to the Flatheads accompanied us. Owing to our lack of horses, most of our men were still on foot. Almost at once our troubles began. For five days we traveled up and down and up and down in steep, high mountains in rain and snow, and then on the fifth day, we had some good luck. On that afternoon we came upon a large camp of Flatheads on their way to go out upon the plains with my people and bought some horses from them. Never having seen any white men, they were at first so afraid of us that the women all ran off and the men stood trembling, not knowing what to do until they saw that we meant them no harm. They then became friendly and held a long council with Red Hair and Long Knife and told all that they knew about the country and the tribes along the trail which we sought. I made their hearts glad when I told them that in the vicinity of the falls the of Big-River-of-the-Plains, the country was black with buffalo and that we had seen no enemies anywhere along that river.

After leaving the Flatheads, the old man Diving Eagle and one of his sons going on with us, we soon got into the roughest, most barren-of-game country that any of us had ever seen [Bitterroot Mountains and Clearwater Mountains]. After some days of it, so great was our hunger that we began killing our horses for food. Then we lost the trail in the new falling snow. Red Hair took some of the men and went on ahead to try to find a way through the great mountains that broke sharp into the blue in all directions as far as we could see. We suffered from cold, wet and hunger, for we killed our horses sparingly. We began to despair. We thought that there would be no end to the mountains, that we should soon have to kill the last of our horses and then, of course, we should die.

At last, after many days of hard travel and suffering, we rode down into warmer country and met some of Red Hair's men bringing food to us and good news. We had no more mountains to cross. A large camp of Nez Perces was nearby, and we could obtain food from them. We made camp that night and there found Red Hair and his men.

The Nez Perces, we found, were in many bands scattered over a great plains country and along its rivers. They had many horses and boats as well, and in every lodge were great quantities of dried salmon and dried camas and other roots. We bought all that we wanted of this food and ate plenty of it, but soon after eating, nearly all of our party became sick. However, sick as the men were and my white chiefs too, we moved camp down the river [Clearwater River] to where it was joined by a north fork and began building boats. Four large logs and one not so large were cut and fires built upon them to burn out their insides.

While this was going on, day after day, Red Hair and Long Knife kept me busy interpreting for them, and that was not easy, for only two or three of the Nez Perces understood a little of my language, and they were all poor sign talkers. The most important news that we got from them was that, although there were some rapids ahead, we could boat down this river into the truly Big-River-of-the-West-Side [Columbia River] and down that to its great falls [Celilo Falls]. White men had been seen at the falls, which were not a great distance from the Everywhere-Salt-Water.

When the boats were finished, we loaded our goods into them, left our horses with the Nez Perces and went on. On our second night down the river [Clearwater River], Diving Eagle had a terrible dream. He told me about it while we were eating our morning meal and asked me if I did not think it was a warning to him to turn back to our people. I answered that the snow in the mountains would prevent his going to them, and he said no more. But soon after we had set out, he and his son got out of the boat in which they were traveling and started up the shore as fast as they could run, and we saw no more of them. I cried a little over his going. He had been good company to me with his evening tales about my people. Now all the interpreting and questioning of the different tribes that we should meet fell upon me. I prayed the gods to give me wisdom to do it. We had with us two Nez Perce chiefs, both of whom understood a little of my language. Through them I hoped to be able to do all that my white chiefs asked of me.

The river was not gentle. We had much trouble in its rapids. After some days we arrived at the place where it entered the truly Big River and then for a time had better water. Then we came to the beginning of terrible rapids and falls along it and twice had to drag the boats around bad places. All this time on the lesser rivers [Clearwater and Snake Rivers] we were meeting different bands of the Nez Perces. At the falls of the Big River we came upon the first of other tribes, people who lived in houses and went about in boats. As we of the mountains fearlessly traveled along great cliffs and across steep slides upon our horses, so did they travel in their boats upon water so bad that it did not seem possible that they could survive its terrible waves and swirlings.

Time was when I should have thought that the people of these different tribes were rich. They had great quantities of salmon pemmican and dried roots. I once had loved this food. I now despised it, and I saw how poor these people were. The only rich people are those of the plains: the Earth House people, the Blackfeet, the Crows. With their great bands of horses they wander here and there over their endless plains, and wherever they go there is their food upon all sides of them — buffalo, antelope, elk, deer — all easily to be killed as wanted.

After passing the last swift water of this Big River, we found it to become ever wider the farther we went. Truly, as a mountain stream is to the Big-River-of-the-Plains [the Missouri], so is that river to this Big-River-of-the-West, just a creek and nothing more. Why, at last this river became so wide that looking across it on a clear day, one could not possibly see a man on the farther shore! And now strange things began to happen. Twice, between sunrise and sunrise, the current of this great river turned and ran back, and the rising, backing water tasted of salt. Red Hair told me that this was because the Everywhere-Salt-Water was close at hand and was pushing back the river water, but I could not understand that. Why should the Great Salt Water want to fight the river water, I should like to know.

We had no sooner set out one morning, I in the bow of my boat, than a fierce appearing animal [seal] thrust its head and part of its body out of the water so close that I could have put my hand upon it. It opened wide its mouth and roared at me, made a splash that threw water over me and then disappeared as suddenly as it had come. It was a water dog! A fish dog! Yes, it had the head and body of a dog but much larger, and fishlike fins where its front legs should have been, and its body ended in a fishlike tail. Yes, and the noise it made was much like the barking of a dog. Red Hair told me not to be afraid, that the animal and its kind did not harm people, but I could not help being afraid. I thought what would happen to my son and me if we were to be upset. Without doubt these animals would at once seize us and drag us into the deep water and eat us!

We had now come into a different country, a country of much rain and fog. That too, Red Hair told me, was caused by the Everywhere-Salt-Water. We were boating one morning when suddenly Red Hair and Long Knife and all the men began to cry out with joy and point ahead. As I wondered what it was all about, Red Hair signed to me, "There it is, the Everywhere-Salt-Water!"

I looked and looked for it but could see nothing, nothing but the wide river running on and on ahead of us to where it was hidden in dark fog from which came a roaring noise. I was soon to know what that roaring was. We made camp, and such waves as I had never thought there could be came roaring and pouring upon us, wetting us and all our goods and tossing drift trees and wood all around us.

That was the beginning of some terrible days of rain, strong wind, high waves and of hunger. We were on the north side of the river. Some of the men went on ahead in boats and on foot looking for a place for us to camp but could find none that would do. We then, on a still day, crossed the river. More parties went out and at last a good place was found. It was on a little river some distance back from the salty Big River. There on a hill in pine woods, the men built a fort [Fort Clatsop] and we wintered in it. There Indians from different tribes [including Clatsops] came to visit and sell us their bad food, fish and roots. Also they brought women to lend to our men. Red Hair and Long Knife would have nothing to do with these women, and that often made the Indians angry.

There were a number of elk and deer around our fort, and the men often brought in some. They were poor in flesh but better than no meat. The best food that we had was the meat of the dogs we bought from the Indians. We soon used the last of our salt, and several men were sent to the shore of the Everywhere-Salt-Water to boil water and make salt. Not long after they had gone, one returned with salt and told about a great fish [whale] that the Indians had found on the shore of the Everywhere-Salt-Water. I could hardly believe that there was so large a fish as this they described, but whatever its size, I wanted to see it and see, too, the Great Water about which the men were always talking. Red Hair and several of the men were to go after some of the fat of the big fish, and I told him that I wanted to go too, as my man was to be one of the party. He said that I could go. I was glad. I was tired of sitting day after day in the fort.

We traveled three days in bad low country and over a high mountain on our way to the big fish. We struck the Everywhere-Salt-Water on the second day and, great though I had expected to find it, still was astonished at the size of it. In whatever direction I looked out upon it, I saw that it had no farther shore, that it went on and on to the edge of the world. There was no wind but still was that great water angry, breaking in roaring waves higher than a fort upon the sand and rocks of the shore! From the top of the high mountain at its edge, we could see still farther out upon it, but still could see no farther shore. But we did see the Big-River-of-the-West running into it and several villages of the Indians that were built along its shore. That night I could not sleep because of the roaring of the waves, which day and night are ever rushing upon the shore.

At last on the third day, we came to the big fish or what was left of it, just its skeleton. The Indians had taken all its meat and most of its intestines. At first I could not believe that those bones were bones and the bones of a fish. Why, the backbone was larger around than my body, and the rib bones curving up around from it were so high that a man could not touch the tips of them with the muzzle of his upheld gun! In between those ribs where the stomach had been, we could have piled all the boats in which we had come down Big River from the Nez Perces' country, and even then there might have been space for one or two more! As the sun looks down upon me, I tell you in his sight that truly that was the size of the skeleton of the big fish. I did not go very close to it. I was afraid. Its ghost was thereabouts, of course, and I prayed hard that it would do me and mine no harm.

Red Hair explained to me how the great fish came to be there. He said that it had no doubt been chasing smaller fish to eat and that it had got into shallow shore water and the waves had pushed it out upon the shore where, lacking water, it soon died. After he told me that, I feared the waves more than ever.

There were two villages where the big fish had been wave-pushed ashore to die, and the Indians living in them and Indians from other villages had taken all its meat and fat. I saw much of it. I saw with my own eyes pieces of its fat that were as thick as the body of a buffalo. Red Hair bought some of it and some of the oil that the Indians had made from it. He and his men said that it was good food. Myself, I did not touch it. I believed it to be bad medicine. All I asked was that the ghost of the big fish would do me and mine no harm.

It hurt me, though, to refuse to eat it when Red Hair asked me to join in the feast. I thought so much of him that I wanted always to do what he asked of me. But this was too much. I was glad when I saw that he was not angry because I refused to eat the fat. I thought over things he had done for me and I for him. He had saved my son and me from the flood at the falls of the Big-River-of-the-Plains. He had bought a horse from my people for me to ride. He had brought me here to see the Everywhere-Salt-Water and this fish's bones. I had given him my bead belt with which to buy an otter skin robe that he wanted and when he fell sick, I had given him a piece of bread that I had long been saving for my son. Best of all I had saved him and all the party from terrible trouble with my Snake people. But I had not done enough for him. I prayed the gods that night to show me how to do more for him, great chief that he was.

We had no real winter, no deep snow, where we were near the Everywhere-Salt-Water. Instead of snow, we had rain, almost continuous rain. It was in the middle of our stay there that we went to see the big fish. After that, game became more and more scarce, and we often went hungry to bed. The men, too, became weak and often sick. We longed for Red Hair and Big Knife to give the word for us to abandon the fort and take our trail back, but they kept saying that we must wait a little longer so as not to strike the great mountains until the summer sun had melted the deep snow upon them enough to let us through the pass. However, hunger at last drove us from the fort. We loaded our boats and set out upon the long trail that we had made the previous summer.

As we went up the Great River, we found that all the people along it — many different tribes — were hungry as we were. We did get a few dogs from them and now and then a few roots. I ate as little as I possibly could get along with so that there would be more for the men. We had no real trouble until after some days of traveling in the rain and cold, we arrived at the foot of the bad water and falls of the Great River.

We there lost one of our big boats and had trouble with one of the several tribes that make their home at the falls. The men of this tribe tried to steal several of our things, to hinder us in every way they could and no doubt would have attacked us had we not kept constant watch upon them.

After leaving these bad people, we obtained from another tribe a few horses and more from still another tribe until at last we had about twenty head. We then abandoned our boats and set out overland and soon came to a camp of a tribe who were as mean to us as the tribe at the falls. We made camp near their village and they tried to steal from us. On the next day as we were passing through the village, the pack on the horse which my man was leading came off, and an Indian ran off with a robe he stole from it. That made Long Knife angry. "We have got to stop this thieving now, else we shall never get through the country," he said. "Yes, we shall make a stand and kill some of these people unless they give up the robe!" Then he ordered my man to tell me to ride on as fast as I could and tell Red Hair and his men to come back and help fight the camp.

I was on a fat, eager horse, and I started him off up the trail at a swift lope. As I left the village, there was a great outcry, women running with their children to hide and men calling to one another as they rushed about after their weapons and prepared to make a stand against Long Knife. Off to my left, I saw a man mount his horse and take after me, and well I knew that if he succeeded in catching me, in killing me, Long Knife and his men would be killed there in the village. Then later on, Red Hair and his men would be wiped out. I had the lead of the man, but I saw at once that his horse was more powerful, swifter than mine. From the start, he gained upon me. My little son upon my back prevented me from whipping my horse to faster speed, for with one hand I had to clutch hard the edges of the robe by which I held him to me and with the other hold the bridle rope. All that I could do was to thump and keep thumping my heels against the sides of the animal!

I did not know how far ahead of me Red Hair and his men were. The trail was through groves of timber and across hilly small prairies. I rode through two groves, across two prairies, and as I entered the third grove, my pursuer was so close behind me that I could hear him whipping his horse. "I am gone," I said to myself, "but I will keep going to the end."

That grove of pines was not wide. I tore on through it, out upon a prairie and up a rise and, topping it, there saw Red Hair and his men not far ahead! I cried out to them. They heard me and saw me and came hurrying to meet me. I looked back just in time to see my pursuer come to the top of the rise and turn and at once ride back out of sight! Then as I met Red Hair, I signed to him, "Come! Long Knife calls you. We are to fight!"

"Yes!" he signed. Away we went toward the village. We topped the rise, and I looked for my pursuer but could see nothing of him. On we went. I expected at every jump of my horse to hear the guns of Long Knife and his men as they fought for their lives and feared that we should not be in time to save them. Then, how glad I was when we at last rode into sight of the village and saw them gathered at the edge of the lodges. One of the men had found the robe where the thief had hidden it, and, after all, the Indians had not dared fight for it. As soon as we came up to them, Long Knife gave the warriors a terrible scolding and told them that we should do some killing if they ever again attempted to steal from us. Then we went our way.

The next people we came to were the Walla Wallas, who had been friendly to us the summer before and were friendly to us now. We got from them a few more horses and had many talks with them through a captive they had, a young man belonging to a far western tribe of my nation. I had never met one of that tribe before. His language was somewhat different from mine but not so much that we could not understand one another. My chiefs, through me, had many talks with him and got from him much that we had not known about the country and the tribes that lived in it. I told him that he could now be free, that my chiefs would take him to my tribe of our nation. He answered that he no longer wished to return to his people. He was in love with a Walla Walla girl and hoped soon to have her. He spoke the Walla Walla language well and so, through the both of us, my chiefs had also many talks with the Walla Walla chiefs and became greater friends with them.

We got more horses from the Walla Wallas and went on to our friends of the west side, the Nez Perces. They had taken good care of our horses that we had left with them. They soon collected the horses and turned them over to us. Red Hair and Long Knife were for packing up and going on at once, but the Nez Perces told them that we should not be able to cross the mountains for a long time to come, nearly two moons.

So we remained there in the low country, visiting one and another of the villages of the Indians and hunting and starving mostly, for food was scarce. We had a lot of sickness in our camp. My own son fell sick too, and for a time I thought he would die. Many of the Indians were also sick, one especially, a chief who had been unable to move for a summer and a winter. Red Hair and Long Knife doctored him and made him well, as they did the others who came to them. That made the people like us better than ever.

Some of the young women were beautiful, so it is no wonder that our men liked them. They would go to the village to be with the women when they could be spared from our camp. There was one young woman, tall, slender, long-haired, who fell in love with Red Hair. When we at last started on, she begged him to take her with us. Red Hair told her he could not possibly do that.

We left the low country and got up into the mountains, only to find that the snow was still too deep for us to cross. We had to turn back and remain for a time longer with the Nez Perces. Finally we made a second start with a couple of Nez Perces to guide us. We had no trouble in crossing the mountains and ascending the river in my Snake people's country that we had named after Red Hair.

There the Nez Perce guides left us, and I became the guide. Then each day, I eagerly looked ahead for sight of my people. On we went, up the west side of the range, through the pass, and down to the place where the summer before we had met my brother and sunk our boats. Not until we arrived there did I despair. I had been unable to find even old signs of my people. I feared that after we had left them the summer before, they had all been killed by the Blackfeet or the Minnetarees when they went out upon the plains to hunt. I was sad for days, as we went on and on and found no signs of them. There should at least have been early spring signs of them at the Forks of the Big River of the Plains. There I went carefully over the ground and found not one old fireplace that had been made since the previous summer. I did not learn until two summers later, when a war party of Minnetarees returned from a raid, that I was mistaken. The party had found my people encamped at the foot of the mountains just south of the Big River and had killed six and taken many horses.

We raised our canoes from the water, opened a cache of goods we had made and went down to the Three Forks of the river [the confluence of the Jefferson, Madison and Gallatin Rivers]. There our party separated, some of the men going north to Bear River to follow it down to its mouth where they would meet others of the men who were to take the boats downriver. The rest of the men were to go south to the Yellowstone and follow it to its mouth. My man and I went with Red Hair, I to be his guide to the Yellowstone. Well I knew the trail to it, for in my young girl days I had followed it many times with my people.

We were not long in traveling across to the Yellowstone and to buffalo. Again we were in the midst of countless herds of them. Again after many moons, we ate at every meal all the fat meat that we wanted and went to sleep at night with no fear that we might starve on the morrow. I said to myself that never again, unless Red Hair asked me to, would I go into that far west country of little game, few fish and few roots! I pitied the tribes that lived there — yes, even those who had been mean to us. After striking the Yellowstone, we went down it to good timber and there built two boats in which to continue our way. A few of the men followed us overland with the horses. Just as the boats were completed a few of the horses were stolen in the night by the Crows. At that, Red Hair cautioned the herders to look well after those that remained to us, and we got into the boats and parted from them. We had no trouble going down to the mouth of the river. There the herders overtook us in hide boats. After we left them, the Crows had stolen all of the remaining horses and had gotten away with them unseen. Now, a way below the mouth of the Yellowstone, Long Knife and his men also overtook us. Again a united party, we went on down the Big River and a few days later, after passing two white men, free trappers, we sighted the Minnetaree villages. Hunters from them had seen us and spread the news of our coming. There was a great crowd to meet and greet us when we landed at the village of the Black Moccasins at the mouth of Knife River.

With the crowd was Otter Woman, thin, gray-faced, so old appearing that I hardly knew her. She threw herself upon me and wept, crying out to me, "Oh, Grass Woman! Pity me. Comfort me. I have lost my little son! He fell sick one night and died before the rising of the sun."

I did comfort her all that I could by telling her about meeting our people the previous summer. But when she learned that I had seen not even signs of them on our way back, she became sad again. She soon died of the coughing disease — of that and of mourning for her son.

After my chiefs had met the chiefs of the Earth House people in a council, they asked my man and me to go down-river with them to visit the great chiefs of the Long Knives. My man answered that we should go, and that made me happy. Wherever Red Hair went, I was glad to go. I began at once to beg pretty and useful things from my friends so that I would have many presents to give the great white chief when we arrived in his village. But that evening my man talked with some Nor'westers who had come from the Assiniboine River fort to trade, and the next morning he told me and then Red Hair and Long Knife that we should not go downriver. Here, the buffalo country where he had lived so long, was the place for him, he said.

"But you can go as interpreter for the chiefs that we are taking with us," they told him. "You shall be paid for going, and some of our men shall bring you all back to this place."

"No, I feel that I cannot go, that this is the one place for me," my man answered again.

That ended it. Oh but I was angry at him! But what could I do? Nothing! Women can never do anything that they want to do, because of their men! The truth was that the Nor'westers had talked my man out of going with Red Hair and Long Knife. So with but little delay, my good chiefs and their men got into their boats and set out for their faraway country. I watched them until they went out of sight around the bend of the river, and then I went off by myself and cried.

So ends my story.

Postscript

The Rest of Bird Woman's Story
(An Excerpt)

The years of Sacagawea's life beyond the telling of this story are for the most part unrecorded and, therefore, unclear. However, according to Earth Woman and Crow Woman, Sacagawea did see her much loved chief, Red Hair, in later years, for he invited her and her son and man to visit him. One fall they all went downriver in the trade boats and lived for several winters with Red Hair in Red Hair's town, as the Mandans and other tribes called St. Louis. Crow Woman stated that they returned to the country before she was captured by the Crows. Earth Woman said that she remembered Sublette engaging Sacagawea and her man and son to go with him as interpreter on a trading expedition overland to her Snake people in the Rocky Mountains. After several such trips, the family finally went on one from which they never returned to the villages of the Earth House people.

As I did not attend the Louisiana Purchase Exposition in St. Louis in 1904, nor the Lewis and Clark Exposition in Portland in 1905, I did not learn until several months ago [1918] that there had been of recent years a wide awakening of interest in the story and fate of Sacagawea, who for something like forty years had been to me an American heroine compared to whom Pocahontas of Virginia fame was a mere shadow. The latter, so the story runs, saved the life of a white man who had been captured by her tribe and for a few winter months kept a small settlement of white people from being unpleasantly hungry. Sacagawea made it possible for Lewis and Clark to carry out their great undertaking to blaze the trail which opened up to civilization half of a continent. Without her unfailing help the brave leaders and their men would have miserably perished in the Rockies or, surviving the attack of the Snake and the Flathead tribes, they would have been obliged to turn about right there and go back whence they had come!

The manner in which I learned of the wide interest that is being taken in Sacagawea is strange. There came to me here in Los Angeles, from my Blackfeet people in Montana, an oldtime war suit — bonnet, shirt, leggings, moccasins and all — and one of its wrappings was a tattered country newspaper in which I read that the Montana Legislature had appropriated ten thousand dollars for two statues of Sacagawea. One is to be placed at Great Falls and the other at the Three Forks of the Missouri. The article ended by giving a brief account of the life of the heroine. I knew at once that it was not chance that had put that old newspaper in my hand. My medicine — ni'ta'tos'im, my sun power — had taken that way to advise me to tell all that I know about our great heroine of the West. Yet I knew her story only to the time she had left the Missouri River country.

However, she has been written about by historians and admirers throughout the intervening years. To have one's deeds extolled after more than a century has passed, when they were hardly recognized when executed, has been the common fate particularly of explorers, for the service rendered must be subjected to the test of time and the benefits derived as a result of the exploration must be weighed before applause may be adequately given.

The only woman who accompanied Lewis and Clark across the Continent to the Pacific Coast during the seasons of 1804-06 did not in her lifetime receive any personal recognition of the services she rendered these explorers during their unparalleled journey to the largely unknown great Northwest. But the century that has passed since that event has brought a keen appreciation of her services from those who have taken the interest to unravel and examine records of her deeds... The story of the part that Sacagawea played in this continental expedition is as fascinating as a piece of knighthood fiction. The fact that it is history also adds to its charm...

Sacagawea's life has two periods: that about which we

know and that about which nothing can be learned. This latter period has been the stumbling block, "the winter of our discontent." We see her in the vigor of splendid young womanhood. She disappears as mysteriously as she appeared...

Her man...Charbonneau received from Lewis and Clark for his services "his wages, amounting to $500.33, including the price of a horse and a lodge purchased for him." There is no record to show that Sacagawea received any compensation by gift or word. It is true we find the following in the JOURNALS: "...[Charbonneau] has been very serviceable to us, and his wife particularly useful among the Shoshones. Indeed, she has borne with a patience truly admirable the fatigues of so long a route, encumbered with the charge of an infant, who is even now only 19 months old."

The finding of letters written a hundred years ago shows that Sacagawea was more keenly appreciated than we had been led to believe. This evidence was first made public by an article in the *Century Magazine* (vol. LXVIII, page 876), containing a letter written by Clark on his voyage down the river after leaving the Mandan village, and dated August 20, 1806:—

Charbono:—

> You have been a long time with me and having conducted yourself in such a manner as to gain my friendship. Your woman who accompanied you that long dangerous and fatiguing rout to the Pacific Ocean and back diserved a greater reward for her attention and services on the rout than we had the power to give her at the Mandans.

No further attention was paid to this woman, not even in the accounts that have been published by those who made the journey, until the time of the St. Louis Fair, called the Louisiana Purchase Exposition, in 1904; and later at the Lewis and Clark Exposition, in 1905, at Portland, Oregon. Mrs. Eva Emily Dye attracted attention to this pilot of the West in her book, THE CONQUEST, in which she has extolled not unduly the devotion of the young woman to the cause of Lewis and Clark on their marvelous trip.

Evidence shows that Captain Clark...had little Toussaint Charbonneau and Sacagawea come to St. Louis, where the boy was placed in a Catholic school, the teaching being in French, the language of his father. We find in Captain Clark's account as Indian Commissioner, an office to which he was appointed by the President after his return from the West, items under date of 1820, covering expense for school books, shoes, and other things for a boy. This account appears in the name of Toussaint Charbonneau. The boy was born in 1805, hence was fifteen at this time. Both of Sacagawea's sons, Baptiste and Bazil, we must remember, spoke Shoshone, French and English....

In Shoshone, Sacagawea's name was Bo-i-naiv, Grass Woman. There is a compound Shoshone word, *sacajaw'e*, which apparently means the boat, or raft launcher, that closely resembles in sound the name that the Minnetarees gave her, Tsa-ka-ka-wias, Bird Woman. In his "Gros Ventre Spelling of the Name, Bird Woman," the Rev. C.L. Hall of Elbowoods, North Dakota, for many years a missionary with the Mandans, Minnetarees and Arickarees, says:

"...So, for some reason or fancy, the Shoshone girl was called the Bird Woman. There is no doubt about this name or the spelling of it. Washington Matthews, a collaborator of the Smithsonian Institution, published, in 1873, a short account of the Gros Ventres people, together with a partial grammar and dictionary of the language, 'Ethnography and Philology of the Hidatsa Indians.' This work is highly commended by the great linguist, Max Muller, who made use of it in writing his book on 'The Origin and Growth of Religion.' The words for *bird* and *woman* are given in place in this dictionary. We thus get for the name, *The Bird Woman*, Tsakaka-wias, the *s* at the end standing for *sh* in English, and making the compound word a proper name. It is equivalent to the definitive article *the*. Anglicizing this a little, to suit those using only the English alphabet and unfamiliar with the scientific sound of vowels, and leaving off the initial *t* sound, which is hard for English tongues, we have the spelling in English, Saka'-kawea. During the last thirty years I have made numerous additions in manuscript to Matthews' book, and also some corrections, but I have no occasion to correct the words in question."

It is now, of course, too late to give the intrepid Indian heroine her Shoshone name, Bo-i-naiv, Grass Maiden, or her Minnetaree name, Tsaka-ka-wias. As Lewis and Clark wrote her name in their JOURNAL, and as it is inscribed upon the various statues that have been erected in honor of her, so must it remain, Sacajawea, [or as increasingly found appropriate by twentieth-century historians, Sacagawea].

Well, as my Blackfeet people say —
Here my story ends.
James Willard Schultz

Appendix

From the Lewis and Clark Journals

The extracts from the JOURNALS given below include most of what the great explorers wrote about Sacagawea and includes their spelling *Sacajawea*. The extracts come from the Elliot Coues edition of the famous JOURNAL, which was published by Francis P. Harper, New York, in 1893.

Fort Mandan. November 11, 1804. The weather is cold. We received the visit of two squaws (Sacajawea and another), prisoners from the Rock (Rocky) mountains, purchased by Chaboneau. The Mandans at this time are out hunting buffalo.

February 11, 1805. We sent down a party with sleds to relieve the horses from their loads; the weather fair and cold with a NW wind. About five o'clock one of the wives of Chaboneau was delivered of a fine boy; this being her first child she was suffering considerably, when Mr. Jessaume told Captain Lewis that he had frequently administered to persons in her situation a small dose of the rattle of the rattlesnake, which had never failed to hasten delivery. Having some of the rattle, Captain Lewis gave it to Mr. Jessaume, who crumbled two of the rings of it between his fingers, and mixing it with a small quantity of water gave it to her. What effect it may really have had it might be difficult to determine, but Captain Lewis was informed that she had not taken it more than ten minutes before the delivery took place.

April 7. ...Having made all our arrangements [for resuming the journey to the Pacific Ocean], we left the fort about five o'clock in the afternoon. The party now consisted of 32 persons...The two interpreters were George Drewyer and Toussaint Chaboneau. The wife (Sacajawea) of Chaboneau also accompanied us with her young child, and we hope may be useful as an interpreter among the

Snake Indians. She was herself one of that tribe, but having been taken in war by the Minnetarees, she was sold as a slave to Chaboneau, who brought her up and afterward married her...All this party with the baggage was stowed in six small canoes and two large periogues. We left the fort with fair, pleasant weather...

May 14. [Following the account of an encounter with a bear] ...The bear was old and the meat tough, so that the hunters took the skin only, and rejoined us at camp, where we had been... terrified by an accident of a different kind.

This was the narrow escape of one of the canoes, containing all of our papers, instruments, medicine, and almost every article indispensable for the success of our enterprise. The canoe being under sail, a sudden squall of wind struck her obliquely and turned her considerably. The man at the helm (Charboneau), who was unluckily the worst steersman in the party, became alarmed, and instead of putting her before the wind luffed her up into it. The wind was so high that it forced the brace of the square sail out of the hand of the man who was attending to it, and instantly upset the canoe, which would have been turned bottom upward but for the resistance made by the awning. Such was the confusion on board, and the waves ran so high, that it was half a minute before she righted, and then was nearly full of water; but by bailing out she was kept from sinking until she reached the shore. Besides the loss of the lives of three men, who not being able to swim would probably have perished, we should have been deprived of nearly everything necessary for our purposes, at a distance of 2,000 to 3,000 miles from any place where we could supply the deficiency. [Sacajawea, as passenger, rescued several items that were washed overboard.]

Note by Captain Lewis: "Which...I cannot recollect but with the utmost trepidation and horror...it happened unfortunately for us this evening that Chaboneau was at the helm of this perogue, instead of Drewyer...Chaboneau cannot swim and is perhaps the most timid waterman in the world...the pirogue had then righted but had filled within an inch of the gunwales, Chaboneau still crying to his god for mercy, had not yet recollected the rudder, nor could the repeated orders of the bowsman, Crusat, bring him to recollection until he threatened to shoot him instantly if he did not take hold of the rudder and do his duty,...the fortitude, resolution and good conduct of Cruzat saved her...We thought it a proper occasion to console ourselves and cheer the spirits of our men and accordingly took a drink.

May 20. ...After making seven miles we reached by eleven o'clock the mouth of a large river on the south, and camped for the day at the upper point of its junction with the Missouri.

This stream, which we suppose to be that called by the Minnetarees...the Muscleshell (Musselshell)......the party who explored it for eight miles...report that the country is broken and irregular, like that near our camp; and that about five miles up, a handsome river, about fifty yards wide, which we named...Sahcajahweah's, or the Bird-woman's river, discharges into the Muscleshell on the north or upper side.

June 16. (At the Great Falls of the Missouri) Since leaving Maria's river the wife of our interpreter, Chaboneau, has been dangerously ill, but she now has found relief from the water of the sulphur spring. It is situated about 200 yards from the Missouri, into which it empties over a precipice of rock about 25 feet high. The water is perfectly transparent, strongly impregnated with sulphur, and we suspect iron also, as the color of the hills and bluffs in the neighborhood indicates the presence of that metal....

June 19. ...We caught a number of white fish, but no catfish or trout. Our poor Indian woman, who had recovered so far as to walk out, imprudently ate a quantity of the white-apple (*Psoralea esculenta*), which, with some dried fish, occasioned a return of her fever.

June 20. I [Lewis] rebuked Sharbono severely for suffering her [Sacajawea] to indulge herself in such food, he being privy to it and having been previously told what she must only eat.

June 28-29. ...At Portage creek, Captain Clark completed the cache, in which we deposited whatever we could spare from our baggage; some ammunition, provisions, books, the specimens of plants and minerals, and a draught of the (Missouri) river from its entrance (into the Mississippi) to Fort Mandan. After closing it, he broke up the camp, and took all the remaining baggage to the high plain, about three miles. Portage creek has risen considerably in consequence of the rain; the water has become of a deep crimson color, and ill tasted. He...proceeded to Willow run, where he camped for the night. Here the party made a supper on two buffalo which they killed on the way; but passed the night in the rain, with a high wind from the southwest. In the morning...

...finding it impossible to reach the upper end of the portage with the present load, in consequence of the state of the road after the rain, he sent back nearly all his party to bring on the articles which had been left yesterday. Having lost some notes and remarks which he had made on first ascending the river, he determined to go up to the Whitebear islands along its banks, in order to supply the deficiency. He left one man to guard the baggage, and went on to the falls, accompanied by his servant York, Chaboneau, and his wife with her young child.

On his arrival there he observed a very dark cloud rising in the west, which threatened rain, and looked around for some shelter; but could find no place where the party would be secure from being blown into the river, if the wind should prove as violent as it sometimes does in the plains. At length, about a quarter of a mile above the falls, he found a deep ravine, where there were some shelving rocks under which he took refuge. They were on the upper side of the ravine near the river, perfectly safe from rain, and therefore laid down their guns, compass, and other articles which they carried with them. The shower was at first moderate; then it increased to a heavy rain, the effects of which they did not feel; but soon after, a torrent of rain and hail descended. The rain seemed to fall in a solid mass, and instantly, collecting in the ravine, came rolling down in a dreadful current, carrying the mud, rocks, and everything that opposed it. Captain Clark fortunately saw it a moment before it reached them, and springing up with his gun and shot pouch in his left hand, with his right clambered up the steep bluff, pushing on the Indian woman with the child in her arms. Her husband, too, had seized her hand and was pulling her up the hill, but he was so terrified at the danger that (he remained frequently motionless, and) but for Captain Clark, himself and wife and child would have been lost. So instantaneous was the rise of water that, before Captain Clark had reached his gun and begun to ascend the bank, the water was up to his waist, and he could scarcely get up faster than it rose, until it reached a height of 15 feet, with a furious current, which, had they waited a moment longer, would have swept them into the river just above the Great Falls, down which they must inevitably have been precipitated. They reached the plain in safety and found York, who had separated from them just before the storm to hunt some buffalo, and was now returning to his master. They had been obliged to escape so rapidly that Captain Clark lost his compass (i.e., circumferentor) and umbrella, Chaboneau left his gun, (with Captain Lewis's wiping rod), shot pouch and tomahawk, and the Indian woman had just time to grasp her child, before the net in which it lay at her feet was carried down the current.

July 28. [In Camp on the Jefferson River, one mile above its confluence with the Madison]...Sacajawea, our Indian woman, informs us that we are camped upon the precise spot where her countrymen, the Snake Indians, had their huts five years ago when the Minnetarees of Knife River first came in sight of them, and from which they hastily retreated three miles up the Jefferson and concealed themselves in the woods. The Minnetarees, however, pursued and attacked them, killed four men, as many women and a number of boys, and made prisoners of four other boys and all the females, of whom Sacajawea was one. She does not, however, show any distress at these recollections, or any joy at the prospect of being restored to her country; for she seems to possess the folly or the philosophy of not suffering her feelings to extend beyond the anxiety of having plenty to eat and a few trinkets to wear.

July 30. ...having made all the observations necessary to fix the longitude, we reloaded our canoes and began to ascend Jefferson river...The islands are unusually numerous. On the right are high plains, occasionally forming cliffs of rocks and hills; while the left is an extensive low ground and prairie, intersected by a number of bayous or channels falling into the river. Captain Lewis, who had walked through it with Chaboneau, his wife, and two invalids, joined us at dinner, a few miles above our camp. Here the Indian woman said was the place where she had been made prisoner. The [Snake] men being too few to contend with the Minnetarees, mounted their horses and fled as soon as the attack began. The women and children dispersed, and Sacajawea, as she was crossing at a shoal place, was overtaken in the middle of the river by her pursuers...

August 8. ...On our right is the high point of a plain, which our Indian woman recognizes as the place called the Beaver's Head, from a supposed resemblance to that object. This, she says, is not far from the summer retreat of her countrymen, which is on the river beyond the mountains, running to the west. She is therefore certain that we shall meet them either on this river, or on that immediately west of its source, which, judging from its present size, cannot be far distant. Persuaded of the absolute necessity of procuring horses to cross the mountains, it was determined that one of us should proceed in the morning to the head of the river, and penetrate the mountains until he found the Shoshones, or some other nation, who could assist us in transporting our baggage, the greater part of which we should be compelled to leave without the aid of horses.

August 14. "I [Clark] checked our interpreter for striking his woman at their dinner."

August 17. ...On setting out at seven o'clock, Captain Clark, with Chaboneau and his wife, walked on shore; but they had not gone more than a mile when Captain Clark saw Sacajawea, who was with her husband 100 yards ahead, begin to dance and show every mark of the most extravagant joy, turning round to him and pointing to several Indians, whom he now saw advancing on horseback, sucking her fingers at the same time, to indicate that they were of her native tribe. As they advanced Captain Clark discovered among them Drewyer dressed like an Indian, from whom he learned the situation of the (Lewis) party. While the boats were performing the circuit, he went toward the forks with the Indians, who, as they went along, sang aloud with the greatest appearance of delight.

We soon drew near the camp, and just as we approached it a woman [Leaping Fish Woman] made her way through the crowd toward Sacajawea; recognizing each other, they embraced with the most tender affection. The meeting of these two young women had in it something peculiarly touching, not only from the ardent manner in which their feelings were expressed, but also from the real interest of their situation. They had been companions in childhood; in the war with the Minnetarees they had both been taken prisoners in the same battle; they had shared and softened the rigors of their captivity till one of them had escaped from the Minnetarees, with scarce a hope of ever seeing her friend relieved from the hands of her enemies. While Sacajawea was renewing among the women the friendship of former days, Captain Clark went on and was received by Captain Lewis and the chief [Too-et-te-con'l or Black Bow, *aka* Ka-me-ah-wah or Cameahwait].... who, after the first embraces and salutations were over, conducted him [Clark] to a sort of circular shade or tent of willows. Here he was seated on a white robe, and the chief immediately tied in his hair six small shells resembling pearls, an ornament highly valued by these people, who procure them in the course of trade from the sea-coast. The moccasins of the whole party were then taken off, and after much ceremony the smoke began. After this the conference was to be opened. Glad of an opportunity to be able to converse more intelligibly, Sacajawea was sent for; she came into the tent, sat down, and was beginning to interpret, when, in the person of Cameahwait, she recognized her brother. She instantly jumped up and ran and embraced him, throwing over him her blanket and weeping profusely. The chief himself was moved, though not in the same degree. After conversation between them she resumed her seat and attempted to interpret for us; but her new situation seemed to overpower her, and she was frequently interrupted by her tears. After the council was finished the unfortunate woman learned that all her family were dead except two brothers, one of whom was absent, and a son of her eldest sister [Red Willow Woman], a small boy [Deer Robe], who was immediately adopted by her.

August 24. ...They [the Shoshones] now said that they had no more horses for sale; and as we now had nine of our own, two hired horses, and a mule, we began loading them as heavily as was prudent, placing the rest on the shoulders of the Indian women, and left our camp at twelve o'clock. We were all on foot, except Sacajawea, for whom her husband had purchased a horse with some articles which we gave him for that purpose.

August 25. ...While at dinner we learned by means of Sacajawea that the young men who left us this morning carried a request from their chief that the village would break camp and meet this party tomorrow, when they would all go down the Missouri into the buffalo country. Alarmed at this new caprice of the Indians, which, if not counteracted, threatened to leave ourselves and our baggage in the mountains, or even if we reached the waters of the Columbia, to prevent our obtaining horses to go further, Captain Lewis immediately called the three chiefs together. After smoking a pipe he asked if they were men of their word, and if we could rely on their promises. They readily answered in the affirmative. He then asked if they had not agreed to assist us in carrying our baggage across the mountains. To this also they answered yes. "Why then," said he, "have you requested your people to meet us tomorrow where it will be impossible for us to trade for horses, as you promised we should? If," he continued, "you had not promised to help us in transporting our goods across the mountains, we should not have attempted it, but have returned down the river; after which no white men would ever have come into your country. If you wish the whites to be your friends, to bring you arms, and to protect you from your enemies, you should never promise what you do not intend to perform. When I first met you, you doubted what I said, yet you afterward saw that I told you the truth. How, therefore, can you doubt what I tell you now? You see that I divide amongst you the meat which my hunters kill, and I promise to give to all who assist us a share of whatever we have to eat. If, therefore, you intend to keep your promise, send one of your young men immediately to order the people to remain at the village until we arrive." The two inferior chiefs then said that they had wished to keep their word to assist us; that they had not sent for the people, but on the contrary had disapproved of that measure, which was done wholly by the first chief. Cameahwait remained silent for a long time; at last he said that he knew that he had done wrong, but that, seeing his people all in want of provisions, he had wished to hasten their departure for the country where their wants might be supplied. He, however, now declared that, having passed his word, he would never violate it, and counter-orders were immediately sent to the village by a young man, to whom we gave a handkerchief, in order to insure dispatch and fidelity.

This difficulty being now adjusted, our march was now resumed with an unusual degree of alacrity on the part of the Indians.

August 26. In their [the Shoshones'] domestic economy the man is equally sovereign. He is the sole proprietor of his wives and daughters, and can barter them away or dispose of them in any manner he may think proper... A plurality of wives is very common; but these are not generally sisters, as among the Minnetarees and Mandans, but are purchased of different fathers. The infant daughters are often betrothed by the father to men who are grown, either for themselves or their sons, for whom they are desirous of providing wives. The compensation to the father is usually made in horses or mules; and the girl remains with her parents till the age of puberty, which is thirteen or fourteen, when she is surrendered to her husband. At the same time the father often makes a present to the husband equal to that he had formerly received as the price of his daughter, though this return is optional with her parent. Sacajawea had been contracted for in this way before she had been taken prisoner, and when we brought her back her betrothed [Little Mountain] was still living. Although he was double the age of Sacajawea and had two other wives, he claimed her; but on finding that she had a child by her new husband, Chaboneau, he relinquished his pretensions and said he did not want her.

November 3. ...[having made camp near what was by 1918 Fisher's Landing on the Columbia.] A canoe soon arrived from the village at the foot of the last rapid, with an Indian and his family, consisting of a wife, three children, and a woman who had been taken a prisoner from the Snake Indians, living on a river from the south, which we afterward found to be the Multnomah. Sacajawea was immediately introduced to her, in hopes that, being a Snake Indian, they might understand each other; but their language was not sufficiently intelligible to permit them to converse together.

November 20. [near the Pacific Ocean]...we were overtaken by several Indians, who gave us dried sturgeon and wappa-too-roots and soon met several parties of Chinooks returning from the camp. When we arrived there we found many Chinooks; two of them being chiefs, we went through the ceremony of giving to each a medal, and to the most distinguished a flag. Their names were Comcommoly and Chillahlawil. One of the Indians had a robe made of two sea-otter skins, the fur of which was the most beautiful we had ever seen. The owner at first resisted every temptation to part with it, but at length could not resist the offer of a belt of blue beads which Chaberneau's wife wore around her waist.

November 30. ... Several of the men complain of disorders of their bowels, which can be ascribed only to their diet of pounded fish mixed with salt water; they are therefore directed to use for that purpose the fresh water above the point. The squar [Sacajawea] gave me [Clark] a piece of bread made of flour which she had reserved for her child and carefully kept until this time, which had unfortunately got wet and a little sour — this bread I eate with great satisfaction, it being the only mouthful I had tasted for several months past. The hunters had seen three elk, but could not obtain any of them; they however brought in three hawks, and a few black ducks (coots, *Fulica americana*) of a species common in the United States.

December 25 We were awaked at daylight by a discharge of firearms, which was followed by a song from the men, as a compliment to us on the return of Christmas, which we have always been accustomed to observe as a day of rejoicing. After breakfast we divided our remaining stock of tobacco, which amounted to twelve carrots, into two parts; one of which we distributed among such of the party as make use of it, making a present of a handkerchief to the others. Captain Clark's stocking would have been full, if he had had any stockings to hang up for Christmas: 'I [Clark] received a present of Captain Lewis of a shirt, drawers, and socks; a pair of mockersons of Whitehouse, a small Indian basket of Gutherich (Goodrich),two dozen white weazils tails of the Indian woman [Sacajawea], and some black root of the Indians before their departure.' The remainder of the day was passed in good spirits, though there was nothing in our situation to excite much gayety. The rain confined us to the house, and our only luxuries in honor of the season were some poor elk, so much spoiled that we ate it through sheer necessity, a few roots, and some spoiled pounded fish.

January 5, 1806. Two of the five men who had been dispatched to make salt returned...They had carefully examined the coast...At length they formed an establishment about 15 miles southwest of the fort [Fort Clatsop], near some scattered houses of the Clatsop and Killamuck...The Indians treated them very kindly, and made them a present of the blubber of the whale [that had been found on the ocean beach], some of which the men brought home. It was white and not unlike the fat of pork, though of a coarser and more spongy texture, and on being cooked was found to be tender and palatable, in flavor resembling the beaver. ...The appearance of the whale seemed to be a matter of importance to all the neighboring Indians, and as we might be able to procure some of it for ourselves, or at least purchase blubber from the Indians, a small parcel of merchandise was prepared, and a party of the men held in readiness to set out in the morning. As soon as this resolution was known, Chaboneau and his wife requested that they might be permitted to accompany us. The poor woman stated very earnestly that she had traveled a great way with us to see the great water, yet she had never been down to the coast, and now that this monstrous fish was also to be seen, it seemed hard that she should be permitted to see neither the ocean nor the whale. So reasonable request could not be denied; they were therefore suffered to accompany Captain Clark, who, [January 6th] after an early breakfast, set out with twelve men [and Sacajawea] in two canoes.

April 22. [near the mouth of the Des Chutes River, having begun the route eastward] Two of our horses broke loose in the night and straggled to some distance, so that that we were not able to retake them and begin our march before seven o'clock. We had just reached the top of a hill near the village [of the Eneeshurs], when the load of one of the horses (Charbono's) turned, and the animal taking fright at a robe which still adhered to him, ran furiously toward the village; just as he came there the robe fell, and an Indian hid it in his hut. Two men went back after the horse, which they soon took; but the robe was still missing, and the Indians denied having seen it. Being now confidant that the Indians had taken it, I sent the Indian woman (Sacajawea) on to request Captain Clark to halt the party and send back some of the men to my assistance being detirmined to either make the Indians deliver the robe or burn their houses. They have vexed me in such a manner by such repeated acts of villany that I am quite disposed to treat them with every severity, their defenseless state pleads forgiveness so far as respects their lives. These repeated acts of knavery now exhausted our patience. Captain Lewis therefore set out for the village, determined to make them deliver up the robe or to burn the village to the ground. This disagreeable alternative was rendered unnecessary, for on his way he met one of our men, who had found the robe in an Indian hut hid behind baggage.

April 28. ...there was among these Wollawollahs [Walla Wallas] a prisoner belonging to a tribe of Shoshone or Snake

Indians, residing to the south of the Multnomah, and visiting occasionally the heads of Wollawollah creek. Our Shoshone woman, Sacajawea, though she belonged to a tribe near the Missouri, spoke the same language as the prisoner; by their means we were able to explain ourselves to the Indians, and answer all their inquiries with respect to ourselves and the object of our journey. Our conversation inspired them with much confidence, and they soon brought several sick persons, for whom they requested our assistance...[Captain Clark] splintered the broken arm of one; [we] gave some relief to another, whose knee was contracted by rheumatism, and administered what we thought beneficial for ulcers and eruptions of the skin on various parts of the body, which are very common disorders among them. But our most valuable medicine was eye-water, which we distributed, and which, indeed, they required very much; the complaint of the eyes, occasioned by living on the water and increased by the fine sand of the plains, being universal.

May 24. This proved the warmest day we have had since our arrival here [among the Nez Perces]. Some of our men visited the village of Broken-arm and exchanged some awls, which they had made of the links of a small chain belonging to one of their steel traps, for a plentiful supply of roots.

Besides administering medical relief to the Indians we are obliged to devote much of our time to the care of our own invalids. The child of Sacajawea is very unwell...

July 1. We had now made 156 miles from the Quamash flats [in Nez Perce country (Idaho)] to the mouth of Traveler's-rest creek [Lolo Creek (Montana)]. This being the point where we proposed to separate... Captain Lewis, with nine men, is to pursue the most direct route to the falls of the Missouri, where three of his party are to be left to prepare carriages for transporting the baggage and canoes across the portage. With the remaining six, he will ascend Maria's river to explore the country... The rest of the men will accompany Captain Clark to the head of the Jefferson river, which Sergeant Ordway and a party of nine men will descend, with the canoes and other articles deposited there. Captain Clark's party, which will then be reduced to ten (men and Sacajawea), will proceed to the Yellowstone, at its nearest approach to the Three Forks of the Missouri. There he will build canoes, go down that river with seven of his party, and wait at its mouth till the rest of the party join him.

July 6. ...In the afternoon we [Clark's party] passed along the hillside north of the creek, till, in the course of six miles, we entered an extensive plain. Here the tracks of the Indians scattered so much that we could no longer pursue the road; but Sacajaweah recognized the plain immediately. She had traveled it often during her childhood and informed us that it was the great resort of the Shoshones, who came for the purpose of gathering quamash and cows [couse], and of taking beaver, with which the plain abounded; that Glade Creek was a branch of Wisdom River; and that on reaching the higher part of the plain we should see a gap in the mountains on the course to our canoes [which had been cached August 20, 1805, at the Two Forks of Jefferson River], and from that gap a high point of mountain covered with snow.

July 14. He [Clark] crossed Gallatin river ...they reached a low but firm island, extending nearly in the course they desired to follow. The squaw [Sacajawea] now assured Captain Clark that the large road from Medicine (Sun) river to the gap (Bozeman Pass) they were seeking crossed the upper part of this plain and reached the main channel of the river (i.e., the West Gallatin), which is still navigable for canoes, though much divided and dammed up by multitudes of beaver. (Sacajawea's knowledge was extensive and accurate.) Having forded this river, they passed through a little skirt of cottonwood to a low open plain, where they dined. They saw elk, deer, and antelope, and in every direction the roads made by the buffalo, as well as some old signs of them. The squaw informed them that a few years ago these animals were numerous, not only here, but even to the sources of Jefferson river, but of late they have disappeared; for the Shoshones, being fearful of going west of the mountains, have hunted this country with the more activity, and of course driven the buffalo from their usual haunts. After dinner the party continued, inclining to the south of east, through an open level plain (in passing which Middle Creek was crossed), till at the distance of twelve miles they reached the three forks of (East) Gallatin River. On crossing the southerly branch (Bozeman Creek), they fell into the buffalo-road described by the squaw, which led them up the middle branch (main East Gallatin River) for two miles...

August 17. The principal chiefs of the Minnetarees came down to bid us farewell, as none of them could be prevailed upon to go with us. This circumstance induced our interpreter, Chaboneau, with his wife and child, to remain here, as he could be no longer useful. Notwithstanding our offers to take him to the United States, he said that he had there no acquaintance and no chance of making a livelihood; and that he preferred remaining among the Indians. This man has been very serviceable to us, and his wife was particularly useful among the Shoshones. Indeed, she has borne with a patience truly admirable the fatigues of so long a route, encumbered with the charge of an infant, who is even now only 19 months old. We therefore paid Charboneau his wages, amounting to $500.33, including the price of a horse and lodge purchased for him...

January 15, 1807, City of Washington [D.C.]; Muster Roll of Lewis and Clark's Corp of Discovery:
...32. Sacajawea, Bird-woman, with her infant, born Feb. 11th, 1805...With rispect to all those persons whose names are entered on this roll, I feel a peculiar pleasure in declaring, that the ample support which they gave us under every difficulty, the manly firmness which they evinced on every necessary occasion, and the patience and fortitude, with which they submitted to and bore the fatigues and painful sufferings incident to my late tour to the Pacific Ocean entitles them to my warmest approbation and thanks, nor will I suppress the expression of a hope that the recollection of services thus faithfully performed will meet a just reward...

(Signed) Meriwether Lewis Capt.
1st. U.S. Regt. Infty.

ABOUT THE AUTHOR
JAMES WILLARD SCHULTZ

On a hot July day in 1877, a seventeen year-old lad from Boonesville, New York, walked off the gangplank of a Missouri river steamer onto the soil of Montana at Fort Benton. With this footfall, James Willard Schultz entered a wholly new life.

He had read of the Lewis and Clark expedition and of George Catlin's eight years in the wild west. Through these and other readings, he had schooled himself in the ways of western exploration and adventure. Now, having abandoned the private school he'd been attending in the east, he sought a truly experiential means of learning.

Within two days of arriving at Fort Benton, he found himself riding with a group of Pi-kun'-i Blackfeet towards a long dreamed of buffalo hunt...and towards what would become a lifelong involvement with the Blackfeet. He was also setting out on a trail that would, in time, lead to his becoming one of America's best known western writers.

As a buffalo hunter, trader, rancher and guide to the region that would eventually become Glacier National Park, Schultz would spend the next twenty-five years in northwestern Montana. In 1903, following the death of his Blackfeet wife Natahki and the earlier ending of his beloved buffalo days, he exiled himself to California, where he began to write. What resulted over a period of thirty-five years were thirty-seven books, all but two published by Houghton Mifflin, and numerous articles in such publications as *Forest and Stream, American Boy, Frontier Magazine* and *Youth's Companion*.

Having become by 1947 a favorite storyteller of the American West for millions of readers, Schultz died at the age of eighty-seven. His final journey took him back to Montana where he was laid to rest near the bottom of a buffalo jump in the homeland of the Blackfeet...the place he too had called "home."

INDEX

Other Titles Published by Mountain Meadow Press

CLEARWATER COUNTRY! THE TRAVELER'S HISTORICAL AND RECREATIONAL GUIDE; LEWISTON, IDAHO — MISSOULA, MONTANA, Borg Hendrickson and Linwood Laughy.

IN PURSUIT OF THE NEZ PERCES: THE NEZ PERCE WAR OF 1877, as reported by O.O. Howard, Duncan McDonald and Chief Joseph.

IN THE HEART OF THE BITTERROOT MOUNTAINS: THE STORY OF THE CARLIN HUNTING PARTY OF 1893, Abraham L. A. Himmelwright.

THAT ALL PEOPLE MAY BE ONE PEOPLE, SEND RAIN TO WASH THE FACE OF THE EARTH, Chief Joseph.

Write for a free catalog:

Mountain Meadow Press
P.O. Box 447
Kooskia ID 83539-0447